Stories *from the* Heart

Lions Serving the World One Person at a Time

By Robert S. Littlefield, Ph.D.
Director and Professor
Nicholson School of Communication and Media
University of Central Florida
Orlando, Florida

Past International Director, 2014-2016
Past LCIF Trustee, 2016-2019

authorHOUSE®

AuthorHouse™
1663 Liberty Drive
Bloomington, IN 47403
www.authorhouse.com
Phone: 833-262-8899

Published by AuthorHouse   06/17/2024

ISBN: 978-1-5462-1951-4 (sc)
ISBN: 978-1-5462-1952-1 (hc)
ISBN: 978-1-5462-1950-7 (e)

Library of Congress Control Number: 2017918526

Stories from the Heart:
Lions Serving the World One Person at a Time

By Robert S. Littlefield, Ph.D.
Director and Professor
Nicholson School of Communication and Media
University of Central Florida
Orlando, Florida

Past International Director, 2014-2016
Past LCIF Trustee, 2016-2019

Dedication

This book is dedicated to the Lions of the world who for over one hundred years have served the needs of the blind and vulnerable, as well as those affected by natural disasters, war, and disease. Their stories of service from the heart inspire and motivate as we seek to make the world a better place for generations to come.

Table of Contents

List of Tables

List of Figures

Foreword

Everyone has a story. When this book was written, my purpose was to reveal the motivation felt by volunteers who prioritized serving the needs of others over themselves. As a volunteer and member of Lions International, I knew my story of service and I wanted to see if others shared a similar story. I expected that the stories might be different from my own, but I was mistaken.

What I found through the hundreds of stories gathered from Lions around the world was a shared story—a culture of service—and a worldview with the inherent strength to overcome any obstacles that might disrupt a commitment to prioritize the needs of others. Not for political or economic gain, or religious or military dominance, for over a century Lions have chosen to serve rather than to rule to meet the humanitarian needs of others and to bring international understanding to the world. That is why *Stories of the Heart* remains as a testament to the aspirations of a group of Chicago businessmen who formed an association with the goal of serving the world one person at a time.

The first edition of this book was my Centennial Legacy Project dedicated to celebrating the founding of what has become the world's largest service organization spread across 200 countries and territories globally. The project represented for me an opportunity to record and share the experiences of Lions who joined this organization and accepted the culture of Lionism, the culture of servant leadership. This personal goal remains relevant in this new edition because it provides insight into how Lions may have drawn upon their commitment to service while navigating the disruptions resulting from the COVID-19 pandemic and its global impacts on the world.

In 2017, Lions Club members returned to Chicago—the birthplace of the Association—for the 100th International Convention to celebrate the Centennial and recommit to the principles of the founders, launching a Second Century of Service. New initiatives expanded global causes, a major capital campaign for Lions Clubs International Foundation (LCIF) began, and the first woman in the Association's history elected to the executive leadership group, was ready to lead the association in 2018-2019. The future was bright with possibilities for growth and an annual goal to serve 500+ million people around the globe motivated Lions to recruit new members and expand their efforts.

Then, in 2020, the COVID-19 pandemic struck the world and because Lions offer their services through human interaction, Lions Clubs were forced to alter their local operations and Lions International faced the challenge of how to maintain its global organization and provide service in this new pandemic environment. Would Lions rise to the challenge? Could they find ways to serve without threatening their own health and well-being? Fast forward, the answer is yes to both questions and the reasons why Lions have been successful in the post-COVID-19 era have their origins in the stories and ideas shared in this book. The reasons why individuals joined Lions Clubs and continued their involvement over time was something akin to a accepting a vocation or a calling to help make the world a better place for those in need.

Using the phrase from the heart was chosen carefully to describe the stories in this book because it identifies a place of origin. What does from the heart signify? Most dictionaries define from the heart to mean being completely honest or sincere about your feelings (e.g., Cambridge Dictionary, 2024; The Free Dictionary, 2024). But there may be more to it than that. For example, the ancient Greek philosopher, Aristotle believed that the heart was the most important organ in the body because it sent messages to all the other organs (A History of the Heart, n.d.). According to Sebastian (2016) some philosophers in ancient times like Archimedes believed that the brain pumped blood, and the heart, controlled thoughts and feelings. For me, from the heart designates a connection to deeply felt emotions, a letting down of one's guard or protective shield to reveal the true self. As one contemporary writer described, from the heart means, "filled through-and-through with love or gratitude or whatever ... The opposite kind of imagery appears in 'off the top of my head,' meaning that an idea is superficial" (Berg, 2001).

Using stories from the heart in the title, to relay how service transforms lives, and creates a greater sense of purpose, seemed like the right choice for a book about Lions Clubs International (LCI) and its impact on the world. Through the stories and comments included in this book, the reader can gain a better understanding of what service to others has meant for those who have chosen to heed the call globally to give of themselves to make life better for others in need.

As volunteers, Lions gain satisfaction through service so long as it continues to be meaningful. As Past International President Bob Corlew reflected:

> I really didn't see the great work that Lions do until I had the opportunity to be an international officer. I have been privileged to travel to so many countries where Lions have done so much. And I have seen some of the people who have been restored to sight because of the Lions. I have seen others who have gotten or are getting an education that they would never have gotten otherwise. I have seen people in pain and suffering who are getting care through hospitals operated by Lions who would otherwise have died without getting that attention. I've seen young people who are becoming productive citizens and who really understand what life is all about because of the work of the Lions. It's truly a joy to be a member of an association that does such remarkable things to help so many people.

This final thought has significance and speaks to the heart of Lions worldwide because, it is truly a joy to be a member of an association that does so much to help so many people. I could not agree more. Because of what being a Lion has done to enrich my own life and the lives of those around me, this book also conveys my appreciation to the association—past and present—for the opportunity to serve. This book was written from my heart and continues to speak to others who have accepted the call to serve.

Blind girl squeezing nose of clown at Medinah
Shrine Circus Lions Club of Illinois 1981

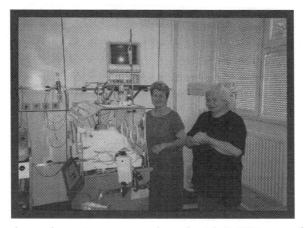

Care given through equipment purchased with LCIF grant funds 1998

Introduction

My experience is happiness from serving; seeing my children volunteering and loving what they do, understanding that life can be challenging, and knowing that it's better to give than to receive. Today we help, but tomorrow we may need help. I love saying, "We serve!" (8:85)[1]

I have seen tears from a grateful parent receiving a basket of food at Christmas, felt heartfelt thanks in a powerful embrace from the recipient needing funds to make ends meet, heard expressions of love from a parent after learning her child would see again and survive the removal of a cancerous tumor from behind the eye, and tasted satisfaction when a fundraising project came to successful completion. These positive experiences touched my heart, and I realized that by helping someone else, my own perspective on life had changed.

How did my perspective change? For one thing, I realized that the more I gave of myself, the more I received. And of course, by using my God-given talents and abilities, I was able to affect the lives of others. While these changes in my thinking may not seem earthshaking, they made me stop and think about what I wanted to do with my life. Now I

---

[1] You will notice that following some quotations is a numerical reference. Because the stories in this book came from Lions around the world—speaking in their own languages—I made the choice to identify them by language instead of by country. In addition, to protect their identities, a number was assigned to each person who provided a response. So "(8:85)" means that "8" is the language in which the response was written and "85" is the participant's identification number. The following language numbers are used throughout the book to identify those who shared their stories: 1–Chinese; 2–Finnish; 3–French; 4–German; 5–Italian; 6–Japanese; 7–Korean; 8–Portuguese; 9–Swedish; 10–Spanish; 11–English.

wonder if others have felt the same way about their service to those in need. And I wonder, more significantly, what triggered that *aha!* moment when they first recognized and acted upon a call to service.

My Story

The story of my awakening to the full impact of helping others stemmed from a time before I fully realized what a lifelong commitment to service would entail. Fortunately, I had role models—family members and teachers—who demonstrated the capacity to help those in need. One of my grandmothers was a quilter and contributed literally hundreds of beautiful quilts to Lutheran World Relief over the course of her ninety-one-year life. But when thinking about when I realized what giving service from the heart was all about, my own awareness came in the form of a prequel beginning long before I joined a Lions Club.

The year was 1967. I just had returned from the United Nations Pilgrimage for Youth, sponsored by the local Odd Fellows and Rebekahs of my community. The experience brought high school students who were interested in humanitarianism and world affairs to spend a week in New York City at the United Nations—attending briefing sessions and programs conducted by ambassadors, international guests and officials, and staff members—learning about the importance of working together in the spirit of cooperation and world peace. Upon my return home, I was encouraged to speak at local clubs and organizations about the trip and what I learned and to promote the experience with my classmates.

It was not long before I was scheduled to speak at the Fargo Lions Club. I did not know the role played by Lions Clubs International when the United Nations was created, and I cannot say that my first exposure to a Lions Club as a sophomore in high school had an effect on what I would say or do when I attended the first debate team meeting of the season. But in retrospect, it probably stimulated my interest in service organizations and in giving of my time to help others.

I was sixteen years old and starting my second year on the high school debate team. As a returning member of the team, I was in line to compete on the varsity level. But there was an uneven number of debaters and partners who had not yet been assigned. At this point, a new sophomore student appeared at the organizational meeting, and she was unlike any other debater I had ever met. She was blind, and she wanted to be on the team. When the coach asked, "Who would be interested being her partner?" I said that I would.

I made the commitment without really knowing what being her partner would entail, especially in an era before computers and advanced technology. I found out quickly that if we were going to debate in tournaments, I would need to spend a lot of time helping her to prepare. We needed to do research, but unlike other teams, we could not share our evidence. On the contrary, every piece of evidence I found in print, including the complete source citations, had to be read to her so she could type the information in braille. Also, every piece of evidence had to have a heading so it could be filed and retrieved quickly during a round of competition.

Despite the fact that she had an excellent memory, keeping track of arguments for an hour-long debate required notetaking, and the stylus she used to print in braille was too slow. If she used her braille typewriter to take notes as she listened, it was easier to flow the arguments and prepare her rebuttal. Unfortunately, when the competing teams complained about the noise of the braillewriter being too distracting for them to think clearly, we had to come up with a solution. It came in the form of a wooden box I built. I lined it with foam rubber that covered the keyboard to muffle the sound. We painted it in our school colors, and we continued debating.

At the tournaments, all of the file boxes carrying our evidence needed to be moved from competition room to room, often in multistoried high schools without elevators. This resulted in the purchase of a collapsible grocery cart. We navigated the hallways with her slight grip on my elbow to guide her as I carried and pushed the cart with all the evidence. While we both wanted to win in the debate rounds, our goal soon became more about what it meant for her as an individual (and for us as a team) to be fully functioning in the competitive debate environment, in spite of her blindness.

There were times when we may have won some debate rounds because the judges were in awe of her ability, and I'm certain we lost some rounds because the judges did not want to show favoritism toward a blind debater.

Through it all, I found that for me, helping her to succeed became more important than taking home a trophy. Fortunately, we were successful more often than not, and even today, some of our former competitors who have remained as friends remember what it was like to debate against us.

By debating with her, I received the gift of recognizing something in myself—the willingness to help someone achieve success—and the joy of knowing that I made a difference. She eventually went to law school and a career in government. While I cannot be sure that what I did by being her partner changed her life, I know that she changed mine.

Reason for Writing this Book

So, what does my personal story have to do with the subject of this book? In actuality, my experience and its story is the seed that germinated into this project to enable others to tell their stories of self-awareness as they learned about themselves and their calling to service. Stories are an important way for people to explain and understand their world and their place in it. Through storytelling, people give meaning to their lives as they describe who they are, why they act as they do, and how they view their place in society.

This is a book about the stories of people who provided service to others through Lionism. Providing service to others seems so simple, yet it is elusive. What motivates a person to serve? Is it part of a person's DNA? Do we serve because we are taught to do so? Does a person serve as a duty or obligation, like something that is job related? Or does service result from an innate need that is seen or felt? From where in a human being does the interest or commitment to serve come?

Some say that people serve because that is the kind of people they are. A Lion said, "I think it's in my character and in my early life experiences as a little child" (5:95). Others tell that they were taught to serve by their parents and family, teachers and coaches, and other influential adults as they were growing up. This influence was expressed by a Lion who commented, "My parents were members of Lions Club and taught us in our early ages that helping others is good for those in need, and for ourselves" (8:87). For some, service is a job that they take very seriously

4

as they shape their lives around a schedule of service to others. A Lion explained, "I work as a public servant, and this is an extension of what I enjoy doing" (11:42). In actuality, many say they serve because they see a need and it is the right thing to do. The words of an individual Lion suggested the feelings of many: "It gives me personal satisfaction being able to contribute even in the smallest part to improve the world" (5:31). Rather than trying to identify one reason that fits all, it may be better to think that there are many reasons people choose to commit themselves to a life of service.

Lions Clubs International

The celebration of the centennial year for Lions Clubs International (LCI) and the fiftieth anniversary of Lions Clubs International Foundation (LCIF) serves as the main reason for writing this book. The magnitude of one hundred years of service and fifty years of funding service projects and initiatives is powerful, when thinking about the number of lives that have been affected by Lions worldwide. As a matter of record, Lions around the world are striving to serve the needs of 200 million people annually through the service they provide. Since the founding of the organization, Lions have dedicated themselves to be what Helen Keller termed, *Knights of the Blind* in service to those in need. With 1.45 million Lions and Leos currently in nearly 200 countries and territories around the world, the motto *We Serve!* reflects a commitment to service that is an inherent reason why people have joined Lions Clubs.

Certainly, the desire to provide service is one of the reasons why people become Lions. But what do we know about how Lions view this calling to serve others as LCI begins its second century of service? This book provides some insight and may help us find answers to our questions.

How the Information was Gathered

This book contains personal stories coming from around the world. These stories from the heart are special and unique to each individual willing to share them. As such, several steps were taken to protect the rights of those who offered their stories. For those familiar with the standards for ethical research with human subjects set by Institutional Review Boards in the United States (American Psychological Association, 2010), appropriate procedures were approved at North Dakota State University and all stories and comments included in this book came from people who voluntarily participated and gave their permission to use their information. Some stories have names associated with them, while others are included anonymously. The association of a name with a comment is based upon how the information was secured; and may explain the reason why a particular person's name is not found in the book. The reason for the name not being included may be based upon the story being provided anonymously through the survey.

The Collection Process

Initially, a survey was created to gather information from people involved in service projects sponsored by Lions Clubs. The survey questions were developed so people could feel comfortable sharing their stories and information. These questions were open-ended and asked: When did you begin serving the needs of others? What motivated you to begin serving? What keeps you serving? How long will you keep serving the needs of others? After these questions, two options were designed to encourage the sharing of stories and additional information: Please share the story of when you first knew in your heart that you wanted to serve the needs of others; and, please share anything else you want to say about service.

To determine if this survey would produce the kind of information needed for the project, a group of easily accessible and willing individuals at a Lions' district convention in Saskatchewan, Canada, were invited to answer the questions. Their responses were recorded and later transcribed. After reviewing the content of their responses and stories, it was determined that the questions were understandable and easy for people to answer. These initial twenty-two stories were retained as part of the story database.

Once the decision was made to expand the project to the international level, I developed an online survey using the original questions, along with some demographic items requesting information about length of service, and anticipated future service. To provide for an international sampling, staff from Lions Clubs International were invited to collaborate on the project. Following the necessary review of procedures, LCI endorsed the project and became a full partner.

Collaboration with LCI occurred on many levels. LCI staff members translated the survey questions from English into the ten other official languages recognized by the association. Assistance from colleagues at North Dakota State University in Fargo helped to format the translated questions into an online survey format called qualtrics. Then, using a random sampling method, 5,000 Lions Club members with e-mail addresses on file at LCI were generated from the 1.4 million membership to receive the survey.

Those who completed the survey responded to the questions in their own languages. This provided data drawn from participants using all eleven languages. It should be noted that those participants listing English as their primary language may have been drawn from countries on every continent, including the Far East, South Asia, and Southeast Asia because parts of these areas were associated earlier with the British Commonwealth. In order to provide a reliable translation of the information, native-speaking college students from each of the non-English languages, with an excellent command of the nuances of both their own native language and English, were paid to translate the non-English responses to English. The translators went through a seminar where they learned about the project. They were trained to focus on the intent of each message and to retain as much of the original character of the respondents' tone and meaning, using appropriate punctuation and phrasing. Once translated, spelling and grammar were reviewed for readability and consistency. These responses were then entered into a spreadsheet so they could be sorted by language, question, and theme. A total of 840 surveys were returned and used in the analysis.

Finally, online letters of invitation to participate in the survey were sent to two groups: English-speaking District Governors serving in 2015–2016; and other individuals identified as leaders serving at the district, multiple district, or international levels of LCI. The invitations to the District Governors encouraged them to identify an individual or individuals to share stories about their service experiences. This request included a link to the online qualtrics survey, where they could answer the questions and share a personal story about their service. Nineteen stories were submitted online from this group. Additional personal invitations to Lion leaders produced thirty-four stories. All of the stories were numbered, and for those granting permission, the names of the storytellers were included. In total, 915 participants from around the world provided data or stories revealing their personal commitments to service.

Not all of the participants fully completed all of the survey questions. However, if the participant provided a story, it was added to the story database. Table 1.1 provides a breakdown of participants by language and age group. The largest percentage of respondents indicated they had volunteered their service for more than twenty years. The number of participants from the languages of the Far East—Chinese, Japanese, and Korean—reflected a lower participation rate. This may have been due to the limited number of personal computers available to Lions in these countries, the number of personal email addresses on file with LCI, or the automatic sampling procedure used to generate the sample to be used in this project. In addition, the English responses may include individuals from this area of the world.

Table 1.1

Participant Years of Volunteering by Language Reported from Completed Online Surveys

	English	Italian	Swedish	Spanish	Portuguese	Korean	Japanese	Finnish	Chinese	German	French	Total	%
< one year	3	3	2	8	5	0	0	1	1	1	1	25	3%
1-5 years	8	13	13	27	17	0	1	14	0	6	11	110	14%
6-10 years	7	16	16	17	13	0	2	15	0	6	16	108	13%
11-15 years	10	8	9	17	9	2	8	13	2	4	11	93	12%
16-20 years	8	14	13	7	16	0	4	14	3	8	13	100	13%
>20 years	46	44	34	45	46	0	29	49	3	26	38	360	45%
Completed surveys	82	98	87	121	106	2	44	106	9	51	90	796	100%

Sorting the Information

The stories from the heart became a major portion of this book. As the stories were collected, they were numbered sequentially. The integrity of each story was maintained, but stories were edited to enhance readability. Where permitted, the authors of the stories were attributed to their stories. Only one hundred stories from the heart were included to correspond with the one hundred years of service being celebrated by Lions Clubs International. The selected stories were chosen subjectively; based upon the *aha!* moment shared, the clarity of the story, and the persona of the storyteller. Unfortunately, many more stories were submitted than could be included.

Responses to each of the survey questions were identified by language and then numbered sequentially. For responses noted in chapter 3, sentences were read multiple times to identify emergent themes from the data. The constant comparison of previously identified and new topics coming from the responses produced a list of major themes that were used to sort and make sense of the information. In chapter 4, the responses were coded using established motivations to sort the responses. In all cases, intercoder reliability was established using percentage of agreement that resulted from discussion to reach consensus when disagreements were found. The responses were then grouped by theme to provide a better understanding of each dimension of the broader category. The nature of the data produced exemplars for inclusion drawn from the different cultural groups represented by the languages of LCI. These exemplars produced a composite persona of those who feel in their hearts the call to service.

Organization of the Book

This book is divided into seven chapters that reveal the call to service, what motivates people to sustain their service over time, and the strategies used to enculture the call to serve in others. Following the introduction, the evolution of service activities as the foundation for the world's largest service organization—Lions Clubs International—is provided in chapter two. Chapter 3 reveals initial reasons why people are drawn and motivated to serve. The factors that continue motivating people to serve and reasons used to recruit new volunteers are identified in chapter 4. To recognize the one hundredth anniversary of LCI, one hundred stories comprise chapter 5, as Lions shared their personal moments when they knew they would always prioritize serving the needs of others. Suggestions for sustaining a commitment to service are detailed in chapter 6; with challenges facing future volunteers completing the book as an epilogue.

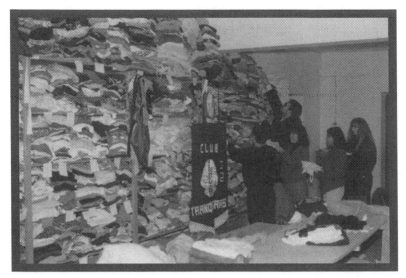

Clothing relief effort in Uruguay 1990-1999

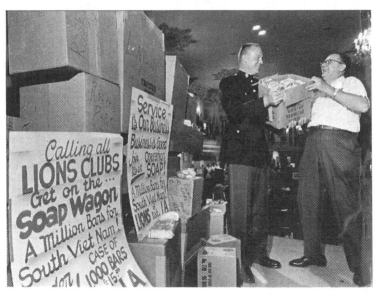

Collect 100 million bars of soap for South Vietnam 1966

Chapter 2

Lions Answer the Call

"Lionism is not a thing to be put on like a badge when one enters a meeting, and to be laid aside and forgotten when the meeting is adjourned. Lionism is a real, living thing, conferring its privileges and imposing its obligations alike; and the real Lion is the [person] who recognizes and accepts both in the same spirit." (President Ray L. Riley, 1929, Kleinfelder and Brennan, *n.d.)*

This chapter begins with a story—Helen Keller's story—and then provides a broad survey of how Lions Clubs have served their communities and people in need throughout their one-hundred-year history. Many books have been written about Lions Clubs International (LCI) with attention to its leaders, its structure, and landmark events. My purpose is not to duplicate these efforts; but rather, to provide a general, thematic review of how the focus on service evolved in response to historical and societal forces. While some specific activities and events are identified, they are not meant to represent a complete listing of all Lions' service activities during the time periods being referenced.

Helen's Story

We all have had a day in our lives that was most memorable. For Helen Keller, that day was when her teacher, Anne Sullivan came into her life on March 3, 1887. The story of Helen Keller and her relationship with her teacher, Anne Sullivan-Macy, is well-known around the world. Paul

Martin (1991) historically described Helen Keller as one of the world's most extraordinary women. The story of how she changed the lives of Lions at the 1925 convention in Cedar Point, Ohio, may be less familiar and should be retold in this book. Complementing what has been written of this event; the following is a retelling of the story with a focus on how it affected those who heard Helen's message that day.

In 1925, Helen and Anne were in the midst of a three-year fundraising tour for the American Foundation for the Blind. The Foundation was established in 1921 due to a growing concern about vision loss prompted by the return of blind veterans from World War I. The Foundation created the Helen Keller Endowment and the goal was to raise two million US dollars, primarily to prevent blindness among children. By the spring of 1925, Helen and Anne had spoken to hundreds of thousands of people in 123 cities (Martin & Kleinfelder, 2008).

While Helen was an effective fundraiser, she wanted to take a break and spend the summer of 1925 in the mild climate of California because she was concerned about Anne's declining health due to the constant travel. In addition, she had grown increasingly irritated by having to appear as *beggars*, as she described herself and Anne. Despite her request to extend her stay in California, the Foundation asked them to return to New York by June 15. This did not sit well with Helen. In response, Helen reminded the Foundation that the Lions had invited them to speak at their convention in Ohio, and they planned to honor that commitment (Martin & Kleinfelder, 2008).

When Helen and Anne arrived at the convention on June 30, 1925, few people in Cedar Point knew they were coming. However, when they entered the convention hall, and were presented to the delegates by International President Harry A. Newman, of Toronto, Ontario, Canada, they were greeted with a standing ovation. As was customary when they addressed an audience, Anne spoke first to tell the story of how she came into Helen's life and ultimately changed it. Anne remarked on Helen's uniqueness: "Few human beings, if you stop and think of it, have overcome such obstacles. Deaf, blind and mute from her nineteenth month, she has had to create a world of her own, with the help of the sense of touch and a great imagination" (Martin, 1991, p. 56).

The story of Helen's awakening to the power of language and its meaning was powerful. Jay Copp, Senior Editor of THE LION magazine, reflected that it was difficult to appreciate how the public felt about Helen. Unlike other heroes of the day—Charles Lindbergh or Babe Ruth—she was not famous for what she did, but rather for who she was. She overcame her disabilities, stretched the boundaries of human potential, and left people with the impression they had touched greatness. Mark Twain believed that, "she will be as famous a thousand years from now as she is today" (Martin & Kleinfelder, 2008, p. 29).

After her remarks, Anne stood beside Helen at the microphone, planning to repeat what she said for the audience's benefit because Helen's voice was often thought to be difficult to understand. But on this day, Helen herself spoke with power and precision and her voice filled the hall. As recorded by Martin and Kleinfelder (2008), she first described herself as *an opportunity* waiting to be taken:

> I suppose you have heard the legend that represents opportunity as a capricious lady, who knocks at every door but once, and if the door isn't opened quickly, she passes on, never to return. And that is as it should be. Lovely, desirable ladies won't wait. You have to go out and grab them. I am your opportunity. I am knocking at your door. I want to be adopted … I hope you will adopt me … What I offer you is full of splendid opportunities for service. (p. 31)

She pointedly asked the audience to imagine what it must be like to be blind. Helen put the Lions in attendance into the position of thinking about what her life must be like:

> Picture yourself stumbling and groping at noonday as in the night; your work, your independence, gone. In that dark world wouldn't you be glad if a friend took you by the hand and said, 'Come with me and I will teach you how to do some of the things you used to do when you could see.'? (p. 32)

Helen's message was focused on more than raising funds for the American Foundation for the Blind. She was calling on Lions to provide service to lift up the blind and visually impaired, and help them to experience a meaningful life:

> It is because my teacher learned about me and broke through the dark, silent imprisonment which held me that I am able to work for myself and for others. It is the caring we want more than money. The gift without the sympathy and interest of the giver is empty. If you care, if we can make the people of this great country care, the blind will indeed triumph over blindness. (p. 32)

Helen closed her ten-minute speech using an historic metaphor, suggesting that the crusade against darkness was a noble cause. She used an appeal that touched the hearts of the 5,000 Lions in attendance that day:

> Will you not help me hasten the day when there shall be no preventable blindness; no little deaf, blind child untaught; no blind man or woman unaided? I appeal to you Lions, you who have your sight, your hearing, you who are strong and brave and kind. Will you not constitute yourselves Knights of the Blind in this crusade against darkness? (p. 32)

When Helen finished her speech, the Lions jumped to their feet and applauded enthusiastically.

Motions were made and seconded to make Helen Keller and Anne Sullivan honorary members in Lions Clubs International. Helen thanked the delegates and said she was happy and proud to be a Lion. Before the convention ended, sight conservation and work for the blind was adopted as a major service focus. It should be noted that the name of the focus was altered in 1976 to sight conservation and work *with* the blind to be more consistent with the desire of the visually impaired to gain independence (Martin, 1991, p. 60). As Martin and Kleinfelder (2008) so aptly concluded: "On most stops, Helen touched people's wallets; here she touched the soul of an organization" (p. 32).

The impact of Helen's message was significant and galvanized Lions Clubs into action. According to reports, prior to the 1925 convention, fifty-eight clubs were on record as having assisted the blind in some way. A year later, that number had nearly tripled to 143. Lions had felt the power of Helen's message calling for assistance to help the blind become more self-sufficient, self-respected, and self-supported.

The story of Helen Keller's address to the Lions in 1925 has been the rallying cry throughout the history of the association. The call to serve the needs of the blind and visually impaired gave a specific focus for Lions Clubs and became the brand by which Lions have been known ever since throughout the world. While assisting the blind as a signature cause has been held in highest esteem, Lions Clubs have defined their service for this cause in a variety of ways.

The Focus on Service for Lions

In order to understand how service in Lionism evolved during its first one hundred years, considering the different stages an organization goes through in its development is useful. Some scholars have looked at organizations from start to finish. For example, Lester, Parnell, and Carraher (2003) proposed that organizations move through five stages: existence, survival, maturity, renewal, and decline. When an organization is formed, it comes into existence. In this first stage, the focus is on attracting and keeping members. Survival is next as the organization pursues growth, sets targets, and builds its structure in order to overcome any internal or external challenges it may face. When an organization moves into the maturity stage, a more formal structure has been created and the hierarchy of leadership begins to manage organizational activities by delegation of authority and a chain of command. Because the maturity stage relies on more traditional and established ways of accomplishing organizational objectives, once the organization reaches this stage its leaders have a choice to make. They can either adopt a creative and flexible management strategy to enable them to move into the fourth stage—renewal—whereby they remain current and responsive to an ever-changing environment; or, they may choose to become more focused on sustaining the structure and practices of an organization rather than meeting the societal needs for which it was originally formed. If it chooses the latter, the final stage of decline will occur, and the organization will cease to exist.

With one hundred years of organizational history, LCI has experienced a number of challenges. To the credit of its leaders, Lions and LCI staff have worked very diligently to keep the organization moving forward and renewing itself through strategic planning. Most recently, the association introduced LCI Forward, a four-part strategy designed to enhance service impact and focus; reshape public opinion and improve visibility; pursue club, district, and organizational excellence; and improve membership value and reach new markets (Drumheller & Cherep, 2016).

Another way of looking at the evolution of an organization is to consider how it has grown. Greiner (1972) proposed four phases to describe organizational expansion: creative expansion, directional expansion, coordinated expansion, and collaborative expansion. Creative expansion occurs when people become aware of a need or problem in society and use that awareness to create an organization that enables them to respond. Directional expansion provides more structure in order to reach the desired objectives. For example, specific priorities are set and then authority is delegated to lower levels of management to accomplish the goals. Coordinated expansion provides for a broader management structure to meet the diverse needs of a larger organization. Finally, collaborative expansion enables an organization to become more inclusive of different perspectives and less resistant to sharing with its members the opportunities and responsibilities of serving growing needs on both global and domestic fronts.

In the case of Lions Clubs International, the creativity of Melvin Jones was stimulated by the need to establish an organization dedicated to providing service to others. To keep Lions motivated, direction was necessary for a more structured, grassroots expansion of the organization. As the organization continued its international growth, LCI needed a coordinated approach. Coordination enabled new clubs in emerging constitutional or geographic areas to benefit from past organizational learning as they expanded the practice of Lionism into their own new territories. Currently, collaboration has provided impact, as LCI is partnering with other entities to provide service to those in need. For example, Special Olympics and the LCI Opening Eyes program have partnered to provide vision and eye health screening to Special Olympics athletes.

These ways of looking at how organizations evolve are useful when considering how LCI has provided service throughout the first one hundred years. Table 2.1 provides a framework for understanding how service activities in Lions Clubs evolved from 1917 to 2017.

As LCI moved through the four stages of organizational development, phases of expansion shaped the service focus of the organization. From a broad perspective, service activities have focused on three areas: the local community, the global community, and specific programs promoted by the association. Because Lions Clubs are community-based organizations, Lions Clubs have served their local needs. Community needs include supporting youth, building infrastructure, and responding to events; such as, natural disasters, medical situations, and economic emergencies. Service to meet global needs include such things as supporting victims of natural disasters in other parts of the world and providing aid to troops and those displaced by war or other conflicts. The specific programs promoted by Lions Clubs International have been those set by the International officers and International Boards of Directors. While vision-related projects dominated, other health related projects, youth initiatives, and environmental efforts have motivated Lions to serve.

Throughout the history of LCI, some International Presidents intentionally included the word *service* in their presidential themes, as reflected in Table 2.2. This followed the adoption of the motto, *We Serve!* by the association in 1954. Other presidential themes focused on service through beliefs, challenges, goals, dreams, international harmony, opportunities, passions, peace, and quality, to name a few.

Table 2.1

Organizational Stages, Phases of Lionism, and Service Focus from 1917–2017

Organizational Stages of LCI	Phases of Lionism	Service Focus
1917–1925 Existence Stage	Creative Expansion	Patriotic causes Community development Citizenship Youth Health
1925–1968 Survival Stage	Directional Expansion	Vision Youth Health Community and economic development Humanitarian needs Patriotic causes
1968–1987 Maturity Stage	Coordinated Expansion	Vision Youth Health Community development Humanitarian needs LCIF Supported Projects
1987–2017 Renewal Stage	Collaborative Expansion	Community-based Projects LCIF Supported Projects Service Platforms Partnerships

Table 2.2

Presidential Themes Including Some Form of the Word "Service"

Year	International President	Theme
1954–1955	Monroe L. Nute	"To Have Served"
1965–1966	Dr. Walter Campbell	"The Challenge for Service"
1973–1974	Tris Coffin	"One Million Men Serving Mankind"
1982–1983	Everett J. Grindstaff	"Share the Vision of Service"
1983–1984	Dr. J. M. Fowler	"Join Hands in Service"
1984–1985	Bert Mason	"Answer the Call to Serve"
1985–1986	Joseph L. Wroblewski	"We Serve Better Together"
1987–1988	Judge Brian Stevenson	"We Serve"
1988–1989	Austin P. Jennings	"We Serve … A Changing World"
1990–1991	William L. Biggs	"We Serve"
1993–1994	James T. Coffey	"Service is Our Responsibility"
1999–2000	James E. Ervin	"Visions—For a New Century of Service"
2004–2005	Dr. Clement Kusiak	"Share Success through Service"
2006–2007	Jimmy M. Ross	"We Serve"
2008 – 2009	Al Brandel	"Everyday Heroes: Miracles through Service"
2012 – 2013	Wayne A. Madden	"In a World of Service"
2017 – 2018	Naresh Aggarwal	"We Serve"

(Source: Presidential Themes)

Because service is at the core of Lionism, the following section of this chapter provides a broad examination of how Lions Clubs focused their service efforts over the past one hundred years. The four stages of organizational development provide the framework to observe how the different phases of Lionism affected the focus of service for Lions Clubs. •

The Existence Stage (1917–1925)

In the early years of the twentieth century, the needs of society compelled service-minded people to come together to create organizations focused on confronting the challenges and conditions of the day. Such was the case when LCI founder Melvin Jones and other early leaders brought the International Association of Lions Clubs[2] into existence on June 7, 1917. Early Lions were often members of several service-guided organizations (e.g., Sertoma, Kiwanis, Optimists) because in the progressive era, the culture of the times promoted selflessness.

In addition to a focus on service, a growing awareness of internationalism due to the U.S. involvement in World War I was present among Americans with the financial and personal capacity to respond to these needs. War raised the awareness of people who saw the contrast between the quality of their lives in comparison with the suffering of those who had experienced war at first hand. The result was the banding together of like-minded people who were ready to devote themselves to the furtherance of human good (Kleinfelder & Brennan, *n.d.*). With the need for people to step up and respond to local and global needs during this first stage of existence, Lions Clubs directed their service activities to patriotic causes, community development, citizenship, youth programs, and health.

---

[2] The International Association of Lions Clubs was the original name adopted in 1917. In this book, Lions Clubs International (LCI) is used for consistency unless other names were used in quoted material.

Patriotic Causes

One of the first service areas adopted by Lions Clubs was the war effort. World War I was underway and local clubs demonstrated their patriotism by selling war bonds, collecting books and magazines for soldiers, and raising funds for international medical aid and relief efforts. They provided recreation and entertainment for the troops and built infrastructure to support local military installations.

Lions found ways to provide personal service. They were encouraged to write letters to those stationed overseas and to undertake projects, such as purchasing bundles of yarn and giving them to community knitting clubs to make garments for soldiers. War orphans and widows were given clothing, milk and ice, and other daily necessities by Lions Clubs.

When the war ended, returning veterans joined existing Lions Clubs in order to provide humanitarian service. Because of their international awareness, these new Lions focused their efforts on helping to rebuild Europe; and often sponsored food ships bringing needed supplies to starving children in Europe. The families of those soldiers who did not return after the war also received much aid from Lions.

Community Development

In addition to supporting causes related to the war, Lions Clubs focused their efforts on improving their own communities. Clubs raised funds to build hotels, community centers, and schools; and worked with other community organizations to construct hospitals, fairgrounds, parks, and amusement centers. Projects such as installing drinking fountains, planting trees, conducting community cleanup campaigns, and supporting local savings and loan banks were common. Lions provided housing, supported school bond drives, restored old buildings, erected signs, and contributed to the proper maintenance of local streets and public highways. The focus on rebuilding lives and improving local conditions resulted in community development.

Lions were encouraged to become active at city, state, and national levels. In 1919, the Educational Committee at the Lions Convention formally proposed a set of Principles of Lionism that became the framework for future service activities. The goal of these principles was to promote cooperation among organizations, public health and hygiene, education, ethics in business and social relations, and peace among people of the world (Kleinfelder & Brennan, *n.d.*).

Citizenship

Lions Clubs promoted the institutions of a civic society in a number of ways. They located or created jobs for those seeking employment; and they sponsored volunteer opportunities for young people to learn about taking initiative and responsibility for projects or tasks given to them. Lions engaged in character building by providing financial support for underprivileged families to enable their children to stay in high school. Scholarship funds and programs also were established to sponsor high school graduates for college or trade school education.

Lions Clubs were aware of the importance of integrating new Americans into Lionism. As immigrants entered the United States during this period, Lions Clubs created free legal aid services, and worked with naturalization services. Finding ways to enable all citizens to fully participate in civic affairs was effective in helping to attract and retain members in local Lions Clubs during this early phase of creative expansion.

Youth

In addition to promoting citizenship, Lions focused their service activities on providing opportunities for youth. They built swimming pools for local children, and health camps for the poor, the blind, and others with specialized needs. Lions Clubs collected toys for orphans and poor children, and purchased school books and uniforms. They furnished gymnasiums and donated to orphan homes and places that served wards of the state. They provided equipment for playgrounds, and volunteered for the Salvation Army around the holidays. As local Lions Clubs reported their service at annual conventions, youth activities were among the most commonly mentioned.

Health

Promoting health was a major focus for Lions' service efforts during this stage of development. Following the devastation of the influenza pandemic of 1918–1919 (Billings, 2005), Lions Clubs provided support and services for individuals and families affected by major health crises. Tuberculosis was an early area of focus for LCI because it was most prevalent among the urban poor and was highly contagious. Some clubs combined their efforts by building, funding, and operating camps for those affected by the disease.

Lions Clubs also directed their service activities toward helping the blind and those with physical disabilities. They began working with the American Foundation for the Blind and provided eyesight screenings for children. Often, Lions Clubs worked with local optometrists and opticians who donated their services. Soon, Lions Clubs were underwriting the expense of eye exams and glasses for needy children in their community. Through health camps and scouting opportunities, they found ways to help those with special needs.

Summary

The first stage of organizational development—existence—resulted in an organization with a broad focus on service. In this creative expansion phase, the founders and early leaders of LCI relied on service projects to draw in new members and make membership meaningful to those seeking to better themselves by giving service to others. It was up to the local clubs to decide what form that service would take. Supporting patriotic causes was appealing to some clubs because World War I was ending and the rebuilding of Europe had begun. Community development projects enabled Lions to help their local cities and towns to become better places to live; and through citizenship projects, Lions Clubs contributed to the improvement of many lives that may have been at risk. Youth programs were attractive to Lions because young people are universally viewed as needing support in order to help them to prepare for the future. Finally, health projects focused on disease, blindness, and those with special needs.

The Survival Stage (1925–1968)

By the mid-1920s, Lion leaders realized that service projects were the best way to keep local Lions Clubs strong and their members actively involved. In the survival stage, as more clubs formed and people were recruited to join them, the benefits of using these local service projects to meet the significant challenges of the Great Depression, World War II, and the Korean War became apparent. In addition, as Lionism expanded into new constitutional areas, the established policies, procedures, and programs of LCI were tested by the reality of cultural differences. It was clear that LCI needed to provide direction for the services being offered by local Lions Clubs.

The Convention of 1925 served as the introduction for the directional expansion phase of Lionism because it was there that Helen Keller addressed the delegates and called upon them to become Knights of the Blind. Immediately, the delegates passed a resolution to create a special department on Sight Conservation and Work with the Blind. This was a turning point for Lions Clubs. Programs and service activities for the blind and visually impaired became the mainstay for Lions Clubs for the rest of its first century of service.

In addition to sight-related projects, Lions Clubs enacted service activities supporting youth, health, economic development, humanitarian needs, and patriotism. During this stage, Lions Clubs began to differentiate between ongoing community service activities and service associated with events on the national or international levels. Ongoing community service projects included those associated with vision, youth, health, and economic development. Service activities that tied humanitarian needs and patriotism came in response to the events occurring in the world during this stage of development.

Vision

Lions Clubs immediately followed the direction provided by Helen Keller and expanded their services to the blind and visually impaired. After her speech, records suggested that nearly every Lions Club provided some kind of vision-related service project on a regular basis.

There are thousands of examples of how Lions Clubs helped individuals, families, schools, and communities to provide services for the blind and visually impaired.

Organizationally, LCI established special weeks to focus on the needs of the blind. For example, one of the first of these events was a Lions International Week for the Blind, held from October 16—22, 1927. Lions provided eye examinations, collected used eye glasses, and funded eye clinics, to name just a few of the projects included as part of this weeklong effort.

As Lions more regularly engaged in service projects to help the blind and visually impaired, they realized two things. First, a primary goal of blind or visually impaired people was to become more self-sufficient; and a second goal involved better educating sighted persons about blindness, especially how to treat a visually impaired person. Lions Clubs responded to both of these goals.

Lions Clubs contributed to the goal of independence by supporting the endeavors of blind people. For example, Lions actively sought to help the blind to establish their own businesses where they could sell items they produced themselves, or operate vending facilities to provide goods and services to the public. In 1936, Lions lobbied for the passage of the Randolph-Sheppard Bill in the U.S. Congress to enable blind persons to operate vending facilities within all federal government buildings (Kleinfelder & Brennan, *n.d.*). Once the law passed, Lions began assisting the blind in their communities, setting them up with newsstands, and thereby giving them the opportunity they needed to become more independent. In addition, Lions Clubs supported the blind in their creative endeavors by sponsoring concerts and musical shows where all of the performers were blind.

Another example of how Lions supported the blind is the William A. Hadley story. Hadley, a Chicago high school principal, was forced into retirement when he lost his vision at the age of fifty-five. With the help of a neighbor, Dr. E. V. L. Brown, an ophthalmologist, he learned Braille and founded a correspondence school for the blind. He transcribed books into Braille and created a self-study program. He managed to keep his school in operation until the Depression severely affected the ability of his students to pay. In response to his need for assistance, Lions began financially supporting the Hadley Institute for the Blind and Visually Impaired.

After his death in 1941, the supervision of the school was taken over by the Winnetka Lions Club and others; and it continues even today offering educational programs at elementary, high school, and collegiate levels.[3]

Lions Clubs worked with blind people seeking opportunities to function independently within their communities through the introduction of dogs, as guides. In 1929, Morris Frank, a young blind man, founded Seeing Eye, Inc., a company whose purpose was to use dogs to help blind people gain greater independence and mobility. Lions immediately endorsed this idea but soon realized that the need was greater than what Seeing Eye, Inc. could provide. Ten years later, Leader Dogs for the Blind was founded by Lions near Rochester, Michigan. Lions Clubs became major supporters of this program, and this assistance became one of Lions' most widely-recognized services for the visually impaired. The Rochester facility became a prototype for similar facilities that would follow in Europe, Canada, and other locations.

Lions Clubs also supported the second goal of educating sighted persons about recognizing the blind as they navigated in society. It was this situation that led to the creation of a universal symbol now in use around the world: the white cane. The George Bonham story describing the origin of the white cane is worth remembering. In 1930, Lion Bonham, then his Lion's Club President was walking along a busy street in downtown Peoria, Illinois, when he saw a blind man using a black cane attempting to cross the street. The man was tapping his cane on the pavement, hoping the drivers passing by would realize he was blind and allow him to pass. Finally, the man made it across the street, but the incident stayed on Bonham's mind. Not long after, Bonham got an idea: What if the cane were white, with a red band around it? If the public knew what the white cane signified, a blind person could hold out the cane and people would recognize the need to stop or watch out. The idea caught the club's attention and they manufactured the canes and distributed them to the blind of Peoria. The club leaders lobbied with the city council and an ordinance was passed to

---

[3] As a note, in 2003, the Hadley Institute entered into a formal partnership with LCI to reach more students outside of the United States, and the Institute is the largest provider of distance education for blind and visually impaired individuals in the world (Hadley and its Partners, 2017).

give cane-bearers the right of way at intersections. Soon, other Lions Clubs adopted the practice, municipalities adopted ordinances, and states passed similar laws. Over the years, this practical idea became a worldwide symbol not only of a blind person, but of Lions' work with the blind (Kleinfelder & Brennan, *n.d.*).

Throughout the survival stage, Lions Clubs kept in the forefront the direction offered by Helen Keller to expand efforts to support the blind and visually impaired. The variety and volume of ways in which they accomplished their service in the area of vision is beyond comprehension.

Youth

Lions steadfastly supported youth throughout this stage of development. From individual club and district projects in the early years, to international initiatives introduced in later years, Lions focused their service efforts on those they considered to be the next generation of civic and global leaders. Lions Clubs willingly engaged in all kinds of service projects on behalf of the youth in their communities: They built playgrounds and campgrounds; conducted contests for school children; sponsored Boy Scout troops for the purpose of including the blind and disabled youth; developed athletic activities like Little League baseball; set up soup kitchens; and distributed Christmas gifts to the needy.

A wide range of Lions service projects for youth resulted as Lions Clubs met the challenges brought on by the Great Depression and the war years. Lions Clubs staged events like *They Shall Have Milk* that raised over 16,000 US dollars to supply milk to undernourished schools (Casey & Douglas, 1949). They organized other activities, sponsored educational programs, and provided books for children.

Lions provided opportunities for visually impaired and disadvantaged children to attend camps, often providing transportation for the children and working at the camps as counselors, cooks, and chaperones. The clubs arranged band concerts for their communities, built swimming pools, supervised playgrounds, paid for medication, furnished eyeglasses for needy children, and collected food and clothing. After World War II, LCI records show that clubs continued their support of youth as expenditures for boys' and girls' activities were reported at two million US dollars and the number of youth projects in 1948 was listed as 13,677 (Casey & Douglas, 1949).

The holiday seasons provided a regular opportunity for service as community Lions Clubs looked after families and children suffering economic hardships. Throughout the Depression and war years, Lions collected toys and groceries and distributed them to those in need. Some of the Lions Club toy drives resulted in the collection of literally thousands of toys and boxes of candy for children. The practice of Lions Clubs providing support for youth during the holiday season continued without interruption.

Two programs for youth that emerged near the end of this stage were Youth Exchange and International Youth Camps. Youth Exchange provided an experience for a young person—16–25 years of age—sponsored by a Lions Club from one country to stay for a period of time with a family selected by the Lions Club host in another country. The sponsoring and host clubs paid the costs associated with the exchange and made sure the young person could participate in the everyday activities of the host family. Youth Exchange became an official program of Lions Clubs International in 1962 and remains very popular, supporting thousands of exchanges annually.

International Youth Camp was another program introduced and supported by Lions Clubs during the latter phase of directional expansion. Camps offered healthful living in outdoor settings and brought together young people from around the world. With an average attendance at around thirty, and with participants coming from twelve to fifteen different countries, Districts and Multiple Districts worked together to launch camps in their geographic areas. Sweden was among the first to offer an International Youth Camp; and the first camp of this kind in the United States was held in Alabama in 1965. The camps offered young people the chance to travel and develop lifelong international friendships; and provided Lions Clubs members the opportunity to serve as camp volunteers, chaperones, and host families.

Because young people were found in every community, Lions Clubs had an immediate focus for their service activities. Clubs sponsored athletic activities, staged contests, organized dances and youth clubs, held field days, cooperated with city officials to curb juvenile delinquency, sponsored parties at holiday times, supported Boy, Girl, Cub, Sea, and Air Scouts and Camp Fire Girls, provided equipment, and observed Youth Weeks (Casey & Douglas, 1949). They found ways to make life a little better for children with special needs. In addition, they created opportunities to expose young people to global experiences.

Health

Along with vision initiatives, Lions Clubs focused their service activities on providing educational programs and improving the health and living conditions of the poor and those at risk in their communities. The Lions slogan, *Liberty, Intelligence, Our Nation's Safety* was used as a call to arms in the fight against germs, disease, and poverty. Lions supported health education in schools. Lions Clubs provided medical assistance, operated dental clinics, and vaccinated and inoculated thousands of people. Lions Clubs also began efforts to battle cancer by sponsoring education programs for the public about the disease and the need for early detection and treatment. Among some of the specific health efforts undertaken by Lions Clubs were anti-diphtheria campaigns; and, as polio threatened the public, Lions Clubs raised funds to purchase and donate iron lungs to hospitals and other health facilities. Lions Clubs often partnered with other groups to provide health services, including the Red Cross, Salvation Army, blood banks, welfare funds, and heart associations.

Lions also promoted educational efforts to prevent syphilis and venereal diseases, particularly among young people. An emerging worldwide threat at the time, undiagnosed syphilis was one of the chief causes of blindness. Lions directed their efforts to promote educational programs to prevent and control this disease. Lions raised funds and presented programs for their communities, sponsoring national hygiene weeks with local school officials. During the 1930s and 1940s, Lions Clubs established syphilis clinics; and Lions who were doctors, and other health professionals volunteered their services to treat patients. As specific needs arose within communities, or as major epidemics and health crises presented themselves, Lions Clubs were at the forefront in providing funds and services to confront the challenges.

Community and Economic Development

In 1929, the collapse of the stock market and start of the Great Depression focused the attention of Lions Clubs on the economic health of their own communities. Lions Clubs developed projects that were unique to their particular needs. As economic conditions worsened, Lions Clubs started food drives, created jobs for the unemployed, supplied coal and clothing for the poor, and planted gardens to supply food for the needy. Throughout the Depression, more and more service activities helped the jobless and those affected by the harsh economic conditions of the times. International Lion President Earle W. Hodges paid tribute to Lions' efforts: "During this worrisome period, Lions Clubs have found a new meaning in loyalty to country … and numerous new uses for citizenship. Lionism has … ably assisted in keeping our respective countries on an even keel" (Kleinfelder & Brennan, *n.d.*, p. 80).

As the economy worsened, LCI experienced a major threat to its survival due to the inability of members to pay their dues. Lions considered quitting their clubs to save the dues money for their personal needs. International Lion President Julien C. Hyer called upon the Lions of the world, "to find within themselves an even greater spirit of giving under times of stress." He pointed out that, "the investment an individual makes in humanitarian service is returned to him a thousand-fold. He urged Lions not to be quitters, not to give outsiders the opportunity to scoff … Lionism must be a steadying influence" (Kleinfelder & Brennan, *n.d.*, p. 83).

Furthermore, Hyer suggested that Lions Clubs provide service to their own members who may be experiencing economic challenges. As an example of how Lions helped their communities, Melvin Jones and other Lion leaders staged a national Lions Business Confidence Week to rally community leaders to the cause of keeping dollars in circulation. As a result of the Lions' anti-hoarding campaign, nearly 600 million US dollars were placed into circulation to help keep the banks and businesses in operation (Kleinfelder & Brennan, *n.d.*).

Everywhere people were fighting to regain the lifestyles they had enjoyed prior to the Depression. International Lion President Charles H. Hatton encouraged Lions to persist in their service: "The period of reconstruction has been started and it is for us as Lions and as citizens to 'carry on.' To us has come an unusual privilege and opportunity. Let us not be dismayed nor discouraged, for we are Lions" (Kleinfelder & Brennan, *n.d.*, p. 95). Despite banks closing, LCI budgets being drastically reduced, International Office staff suffering cutbacks, and clubs being unable to pay their dues, the association continued to operate in the black and the majority of the clubs remained active and in close ties with International Headquarters.

Throughout the Depression, Lions Clubs raised funds in order to support those in need. They purchased groceries for the needy, provided hot lunches for children, and paid for eye surgery. Clubs contributed funds to district-wide efforts, like building dormitories at state schools for the blind and raising funds for a summer camp for underprivileged children. As the Depression came to an end, Lions Clubs International took great pride that it had survived. Lions had met the challenge through service, determining the needs they could meet at whatever level, and setting about to accomplish their goals.

As the economy gradually improved, Lions focused on helping their members and their communities recover and on keeping a positive outlook. Local clubs sponsored community activities, staged entertainment in the form of parties and carnivals, operated concessions and booths at community fairs, conducted oratorical and essay contests, and provided the essential services to rebuild their communities. Lions were optimistic and willing to work to improve conditions.

Humanitarian Needs

A form of service provided by Lions Clubs during the survival stage came in the form of disaster and emergency relief efforts. While the focus for most Lions Clubs was on their own communities, when Lions became aware of natural disasters or emergencies facing other communities around the world, they responded by providing needed support and services. It was this acknowledgement of needs beyond the local community that prompted the International Board of Directors to create the Emergency Relief Fund in 1926 to provide aid to those stricken by a disaster or emergency situation wherever the tragedy occurred.[4] Throughout the phase of directional expansion, when

---

[4] This was the origin of what would be established in 1968 as the Lions Clubs International Foundation (LCIF).

communities faced natural disasters or emergency situations, Lions Clubs were there providing humanitarian relief.

The examples are numerous. From helping tornado victims in Georgia, to reconstructing a Girl Scout camp destroyed by a hurricane, to sending funds to the Tsingtao Lions Club in China to aid the destitute after the Yangtze River flooded; time and time again, Lions proved that in the face of tragedy, they would provide assistance in areas far from their homes.

The support from Lions Clubs was reciprocal. As Hurricane Carla struck the Texas Gulf Coast, Lions in Virginia and elsewhere were already gathering clothes, bedding, blankets, canned goods, and other supplies for immediate shipment to Texas aboard mercy flights from naval and air force bases in Virginia. Similar responses were underway from Lions Clubs in Florida, Washington, and Maryland. Even in Pakistan, within a few weeks, every Lions Club in that country responded, and a check for 1,000 US dollars was given to the U.S. Ambassador. The funds were designated to rebuild a community hall that had been sponsored by the local Nardin Texas Lions Club. Not long after, just as the German Lions had sent emergency funds and supplies to Texas, so did the Texas Lions reciprocate when the German North Sea coastline was ravaged by storms, killing hundreds and leaving thousands more homeless. The call to humanitarian aid was one that Lions Clubs heeded.

Humanitarian efforts from Lions Clubs were not only extended through funds. Lions also responded with hands-on service when disasters struck. After a mine explosion killed 111 miners in Illinois, Lions immediately offered their assistance to the Red Cross to help identify victims. Within a month, Lions again answered the call when a nitrate explosion killed 502 people in Texas, five of them Lions. Lions immediately rallied to provide assistance. In addition, LCI forwarded 40,000 US dollars raised from Lions Clubs in forty-seven states, Canada, Mexico, and Puerto Rico to the Texas City Lions Club to help those affected by the disaster.

The humanitarian efforts of Lions Clubs were not only sought to provide relief for natural disaster victims, but as International President Ben A. Riffin said, "The great flood of Lions' rich gifts for the welfare of his fellow man is directed not alone to the amelioration of suffering and want, ... but to the correction of those conditions which make suffering and want possible" (Kleinfelder & Brennan, *n.d.*, p. 57). For example, as

World War II consumed the world, children were left as victims. Canadian Lions created the Lions British Child War Victims Fund, sending tens of thousands of dollars to England to help care for children orphaned by war. This effort was unprecedented and received the patronage of Her Majesty, Queen Mother Elizabeth who thanked them for their work.

On a different level, as a result of the international efforts of Lions Clubs during World War I and World War II, the international officers were invited to represent the association as one of only twenty-four national and international entities asked to attend the 1945 organizational conference to form the United Nations. Through numerous shows of support from individual Lions, as well as from the Board of Directors, Lions Clubs International fully endorsed the creation of the United Nations and helped to write the UN Charter for Non-Governmental Organizations. Soon after in 1947, Lions Clubs International was granted consultative status on the United Nations' Economic and Social Council, a position LCI still retains. This relationship strengthened the commitment of Lions Clubs International to meeting humanitarian needs on a global scale.

From disaster and emergency relief efforts, to supporting the victims of war and destruction, Lions Clubs responded with dedication and determination, providing funds and services to those in need. The leadership demonstrated by Lions around the world created a natural connection with the United Nations, resulting in an ongoing relationship of dedication to humanitarian needs.

Patriotism

Patriotic service is rooted in what was earlier identified as citizenship. The world underwent significant changes in the years associated with the survival stage of Lions Clubs International. The Roaring Twenties, the Great Depression, World War II, the Korean War, and later the Cold War challenged Lions to sustain themselves and their traditions through principled citizenship and patriotism.

The Roaring Twenties was a time of growth and community development. Nothing seemed impossible. Lions Clubs systematically determined needs, and then rallied community spirit to make the necessary changes on behalf of the citizens of the community. Citizenship and observance of national holidays were encouraged. This encouragement took the form of participation in civic activities and supporting oratorical and other patriotic contests where expressions of optimism, loyalty, and integrity were encouraged (Kleinfelder & Brennan, *n.d.*). Lions became advocates for getting legislation passed to provide for the education and benefit of the blind within their states.

During the Great Depression, as immigrants entered the United States, Lions Clubs provided citizenship training to help them to become more familiar with their new country. When communities looked for ways to better the circumstances of their citizens, Lions Clubs launched safety inspection programs, supported local farmers, started Boy Scout troops for wayward children, and helped businesses to reopen by providing jobs for the unemployed.

As more nations became affiliated with LCI, and as the world braced for a second world war, a sense of global responsibility was more pronounced. Lion leaders spoke of the need for global citizenship in order to preserve peace against the forces that would destroy it. Lions were encouraged to act in ways that preserved their liberties; and to make sure that youth were taught what liberty meant, how youth should direct their intelligence toward activities that preserved liberty, and when young people should work to protect their countries against aggression. The motto *Liberty, Intelligence, Our Nation's Safety* took on patriotic meaning for these Lions.

As warfare in Europe, Asia, and Africa confronted the world, Lions were called upon to show patriotism in their communities. Because Lions came from the Allied countries, they demonstrated patriotism through affirmations of the freedoms of speech, religion, and the press. In addition, Lions immediately responded to the needs of those who were engaged in war by contributing in any way they could. In Canada, Lions began war salvage drives, collecting tons of newspapers, scrap metal, and magazines. They outfitted Red Cross units and sold war savings bonds. In the United States, Lions supported USO fund drives, sold defense stamps, and provided gift funds for service personnel. Lions gathered aluminum and sent forty tons of cast iron and carloads of auto bodies as part of a Barrels to Britain project. Lions entertained the troops, supported the National Guard, and picked up draftees to tour the communities near the bases where they were stationed. Lions pledged ten million US dollars of war bonds as part of the victory funds project. In short, what began as citizenship training in the United States transformed into patriotic activities designed to support people around the world who were engaged in warfare. While all of this was occurring, Lions continued to support their other projects designed to help those with visual impairments, youth, and those with health needs.

Summary

In the survival stage of LCI's organizational development, Lions Clubs were called upon to meet the challenges brought on by the Great Depression, World War II, and the growing international expansion of Lionism into new constitutional areas. In order to provide direction for Lions Clubs in their performance of service during this phase, LCI encouraged Lions to support their ongoing projects, such as vision, youth, health, and community and economic development activities. In addition, Lions Clubs were directed to respond as they were able to the natural and human events as they were occurring; such as with humanitarian projects following natural disasters and emergency or war situations, and civic and patriotic initiatives in times of war. What follows is a description of how LCI coordinated its expansion through the formation of its Foundation up until the introduction of women as members of the Association.

The Maturity Stage (1968 – 1987)

With the arrival of association's fiftieth anniversary, LCI moved into the maturity stage of development, ready to have a greater impact on the problems facing the world. While LCI had the capacity to continue at its current level of vision, youth, and local community programs; with the establishment of the Lions Clubs International Foundation, there was the opportunity for having an even greater humanitarian impact. The challenge of moving the global organization forward with major initiatives, while continuing to expand individual membership at the local club level was complex.

Part of the complexity resulted because new clubs and districts throughout the world required the adoption of policies and procedures to account for different cultural practices and norms. In addition, as the tenets of Lionism spread to service-minded individuals around the world, LCI needed to coordinate its messages through multiple languages to people of different cultural backgrounds.

Just as when Lions Clubs were organized during the initial existence and survival stages, when new clubs were chartered in emerging constitutional areas, club leaders tended to focus their service projects on local, community needs in order to attract new members. However, because these new clubs were joining an international association already in the stage of maturity, there also was an opportunity for recruiting new Lions to be part of the international initiatives of a mature organization. This tension between local and international foci required a more coordinated expansion phase to carry out service initiatives around the world.

Long Range Planning

During this stage of development, LCI began its long-range goal planning efforts under the leadership of International President David Evans. In 1968, Evans suggested that long-range planning was essential to enable the association to move forward in a coordinated way, rather than what he described as "the spasmodic execution of each year's plans" (Kleinfelder & Brennan, *n.d.*, p. 313). He proposed that Lions work together through their service projects to build the *Cathedral of Lionism*. District Governor-Elect Jimmy Carter from Plains, Georgia, USA, attended and was inspired at this fifty-first International Convention where Evans laid out his plans to build a free world, support international friendship, promote law and order, empower youth, promote ethical behavior, and maintain a high service image throughout the world.

From this point on, LCI began centralizing the promotion of broad service goals and objectives in order to motivate Lions to perform service projects. This coordinated structuring of service projects gave local Lions Clubs great flexibility to pick the specific activities they would support. The broad categories also gave the new clubs in emerging constitutional areas the opportunity to blend their concern for local needs with the global initiatives being introduced by LCI.

Over the next twenty years, coordination was needed due to changing circumstances and the influx of members who were interested in different types of projects. For example, in 1972, ten areas of service activities were recommended, including: Sight conservation and work with the blind; hearing and speech action and work with the deaf; environmental services, health services; social services; public services; educational services; recreational services; international services; and citizenship services. While Lions Clubs had been involved in these service activities for years, the broad classification system was intended to reduce confusion and duplicative efforts. Thus, coordination came by identifying areas of service where Lions Clubs could contribute to making the world a better place for everyone, but especially for those with special needs.

In addition, to undertake some of the projects on a larger scale during the maturity stage of development, hands-on service evolved into ongoing fundraising activities for many clubs. Through fundraising events, members without the individual resources to donate large sums of money could generate funds through their collective efforts. In some ways, this collective fundraising democratized Lionism; but it also reduced the individual necessity to donate personal funds to support the foundation. However, the paucity of individual donation is not apparent in all parts of the world because just as the founders of LCI were successful businessmen who used their resources to provide services for the poor and needy, generating funds remains an essential expectation for membership in Lions Clubs chartered in what are characterized as developing countries. In many areas, Lions have been those with the necessary resources and capacity to help those with special needs in their communities.

Lions Clubs International Foundation

As a way to provide immediate financial relief on a global scale for victims of natural disasters or human conflicts, Lions Clubs International Foundation was formed. Originally known as Lions International Foundation (LIF), its original purpose was to provide humanitarian assistance to help the innocent victims of war. Prior to LCIF's formation, individual Lions Clubs responded to such needs by individually supplying relief supplies to stricken areas; and funds to support relief efforts were donated by clubs and districts, distributed to victims primarily through the Cooperative for Assistance and Relief Everywhere (CARE) and other such agencies. LCI soon recognized that a coordinated approach was needed to anticipate the needs of those victimized by natural or human-made catastrophes and then to provide funding directly to local Lions who could give the related services needed to put those funds to use. Consequently, in 1968, LCIF provided the opportunity for Lions Clubs to direct funds to be used for Lion-to-Lion service.

Within a short time, LCIF identified areas of need: vocational assistance, major disaster relief, eye care and research, cancer, hearing, and humanitarian services. However, three of these areas emerged as most important: Major disaster relief; vocational assistance; and humanitarian services. Funds for major disaster relief supported the efforts of local Lions to provide clothing, food, medicine, and temporary shelter for victims. In addition, LCIF directed funds to offer more permanent assistance through the building of hospitals, schools, and homes. Vocational assistance initially focused on supporting educational opportunities and services for young people in developing countries of the world. This later expanded to include Lions Quest and other youth empowerment programs. Humanitarian services addressed broad health issues, including vision-related services, leprosy control projects, fresh water development projects, and the construction of sanitary facilities and other critically-needed services.

What LCIF did for Lions Clubs International was to provide the financial resources necessary to help local Lions Clubs have a bigger service impact on areas of need. Using an equation—Good Ideas X Scale = Greater Impact—Lions Clubs were encouraged to support the Foundation through individual and club gifts. A recognition structure emerged to encourage donations of various amounts; and the Melvin Jones and Progressive Melvin Jones Fellowships identified individuals for their significant financial support of the Foundation. In addition to providing resources, LCIF contributed to the creation of the coordinated expansion of Lionism through the programs its grants supported.

While long-range planning encouraged the coordination of service activities at the club level, and LCIF provided the funding to support projects having a greater impact, Lion leaders continued to support the service activities comprising the backbone of the association in the areas of vision, youth, and health.

Vision

The creativity of the first fifty years of service activities provided the foundation for the projects that continued in the maturity stage of LCI's development. While some circumstances changed for the blind and visually impaired in the United States after the passage of the Americans with Disabilities Act, individuals with visual needs continued to seek and receive assistance from Lions Clubs. Lions Clubs supported eye bank programs, paid for corneal transplants, conducted glaucoma screenings, and assisted with all forms of sight conservation. In addition, Lions collected, cleaned, and redistributed millions of used eyeglasses to missions primarily going to developing parts of the world.

As a way to coordinate worldwide activity, LCI launched Journey for Sight—a 10K walk/run event—and other programs to promote awareness of the obstacles faced by the blind and visually impaired; as well as to involve Lions in recreational activities to promote health. White Cane Days educated the public about how to recognize blind individuals in public places, and raised funds to support local programs to aiding the blind. Lions supported Leader Dogs for the Blind and other dog guide programs by volunteering as puppy raisers and identifying potential candidates. In addition, Lions Clubs built and staffed facilities offering vocational and independent life training centers for the blind.

In short, Helen Keller's call for Lions to be Knights of the Blind continued to direct the activities of the association; and through the coordination of a maturing organization, greater impacts were experienced by those in need of assistance.

Youth

Lions Clubs steadfastly supported youth activities, as Lions Clubs International provided program coordination during the maturity stage of development. Lions served as umpires and referees for youth sports, provided landscaping and supplied materials for recreational facilities, supported school activities, sponsored scouting opportunities, hosted Youth Exchange students, and provided International Youth Camps. Lions often focused their service on making sure that young people with special needs were given the opportunity to experience activities enjoyed by other children.

Lions continued their services on behalf of at-risk children through their involvement with and support of youth homes and ranches. The Individual Opportunity for Achievement Youth Ranch in Oklahoma, the Lions Villa in Dublin, the House of Concord in Ontario, and the Lark Ellen Home for Boys in California were just a few examples of how Lions Clubs demonstrated their commitment to serving the needs of young people.

A significant youth program promoted by Lions Clubs International during this stage was the Leo Program. The Leo Program (Leadership— Equality[5]—Opportunity) came into existence in 1968 as an official LCI project. In actuality, the first Leo Club was formed in Abington, Pennsylvania, by Bill Graver in 1957. Bill asked his father, a member of the Glenside Lions Club, why a Lions-sponsored service club for young people did not exist. The Glenson Lions Club responded by starting the Leo Club with young Graver as its first president. As more Lions Clubs in Pennsylvania started their own Leo Clubs, District 14 adopted Leo Clubs as an official project in 1964. Between 1964 and 1967, the LCI Youth Committee studied the project and voted to implement it in 1968.

Leos formed Alpha or Omega clubs (based upon age range) and performed service projects supporting the initiatives of their sponsoring Lions Clubs. Leos organized charity festivals, worked with the elderly, donated blood, collected food and clothing for the poor, participated in community clean-up projects, planting trees, and staging projects to raise funds, to name a few. The overarching goal of Leo Clubs was to perform acts of service in order to make their communities better places to live. By 1974, there were over 2,000 Leos in sixty-eight countries (Martin & Kleinfelder, 2009).

---

[5] Equality was later changed to Experience by LCI.

Health

Lions Clubs provided ongoing service to meet the needs of those experiencing challenges to their health or wellbeing. While the range of health issues varied, based upon regions of the world, Lions provided services for those with Hansen's disease, adolescent drug users, cancer victims, and just about any other health malady a human could experience. Lions provided funds for research and the development of treatments to combat diseases, provided transportation to assist those experiencing those treatments, and extended their friendship and support to those in recovery phases.

Another health-related initiative that received more attention from Lions Clubs during this stage was work with the deaf. Lions collected and recycled hearing aids, created group homes and living experiences for deaf people, and expanded educational opportunities for deaf students. Gallaudet College—the only accredited liberal arts college in the world for deaf students—was largely supported by the Lions of Virginia, Maryland, and the District of Columbia in the United States.

Summary

As Lions Clubs International moved through the maturity stage of development, the need for greater coordination of service and funding was apparent. International Officers and the International Board of Directors used long-range planning to identify goals and areas of activity in order to help Lions Clubs have the flexibility to identify service projects that were consistent with the aims and purpose of the association. Lions Clubs continued with their vision, youth, and health programs; introducing new, coordinated approaches to enhancing service impacts. To assist with the coordination of fundraising in order to have a greater impact in the areas of disaster relief, vocational training, and humanitarian needs, Lions Clubs International Foundation was established. With the arrival of the year 1987 came the introduction of a new dimension to Lionism: the integration of women as full members and partners in the delivery of service to the world. The next section reveals the process and result of this effort to include women as Lions.

The Renewal Stage (1987–2017)

The fourth stage of organizational development is renewal, characterized by a willingness to engage in self-examination and change for the benefit of sustaining organizational health. The need for renewal occurs when an organization becomes so well-established that maintenance of the organizational structure requires more effort and attention than the cause for which the organization was created. In such a situation, organizations become unresponsive to changing demographics and societal norms. For example, as the length of membership increases, the receptivity of longtime members to changes suggested by newer members decreases. Eventually, the new members may look elsewhere for an organization where their suggestions are more welcomed. Thus, to remain viable, organizations must be open to periodic self-examination and the evaluation of their practices and procedures to make sure they are current with the preferences of a new generation of potential members and stakeholders.

Lions Clubs International has been experiencing the renewal stage over the past thirty years as a result of the opening of membership to women, the start of a new phase of collaborative expansion brought on with the support of LCIF, and by the growing competition among service organizations to attract new members. While some clubs experienced internal tensions as men reluctantly shared control of club projects and activities with women, LCI considered the addition of women as full members to be an essential and positive way to renew the organization in preparation for its second century of service.

The renewal stage was characterized as a phase of collaboration. On the club level, collaboration occurred as men and women served side by side to provide service to their communities. On a global level, LCI and LCIF leaders realized that Lionism would have a greater impact in the world if partnerships were created with other major service providers and foundations. Rather than competition, Lions seek collaboration. The following sections include a discussion of three service areas of focus for

LCI during the collaboration phase: Community-based projects; LCI supported projects; and service platforms.

Community-based Projects

Community-based service projects in the early years of the collaborative stage were not that much different from those of the previous stages because Lions Clubs relied on the same kinds of projects that were familiar to them. Club members identified a set of projects they either enjoyed (such as: pancake suppers, charity walks, or volunteering at a youth camp) or were expected to perform (such as: White Cane Day, collecting used eyeglasses, or bringing holiday meals to the poor), and then scheduled and completed these familiar projects on an annual basis. Once their local project schedules were set, some Lions Clubs did not feel compelled to adopt new projects, despite efforts from LCI to promote service activities, such as World Lions Service Days.

With the addition of women into the local clubs, the dynamics of decision-making shifted. As they offered their suggestions, some new ideas and projects were welcomed and adopted by the established membership; while in other clubs, the new members experienced resistance. Some all-male clubs encouraged women to form their own Lions Clubs and some Lioness Clubs transitioned to become all-female Lions Clubs.

Vision remained a high priority for clubs during this phase, but some of the projects changed as technology advanced and high tech devices provided opportunities for local clubs to support braille literacy. In addition, the KidSight project opened the doors for services to preschool and elementary-aged children as clubs began vision screening projects to detect vision abnormalities requiring further diagnosis. Support for youth often found its focus on providing opportunities for children with disabilities or special needs. During this phase, LCI partnered with Special Olympics to offer eye health and vision screenings to the participants. With the growing world population threatening food supplies and exacerbating poverty, Lions Clubs partnered with the United Nations to respond in developing areas by providing meals and support for the underfed and malnourished. Offering food and shelter for the homeless in urban areas was a frequently-reported project. On the environmental front, local Lions around the world planted millions of trees, provided fresh waters to villages and communities, and increased recycling efforts.

Several initiatives involved contests, building collaboration and competition among Lions and Leos, as well as becoming viable service projects for Lions Clubs to support youth and the environment. The longest-running of these is the Peace Poster Contest beginning in 1988 as a way for young people to share their artistic vision for peace. Later, the Essay Contest was added to provide an opportunity for visually-impaired youth to express their views about peace in written form. The Environmental Photo Contest showcased the beauty of nature in an original photograph. Recently, as Leos Clubs increased in number, opportunities to involve them in advancing the goals of Lionism resulted in the Leo Day Video Contest. In this competition, Leo Clubs were invited to use the Sustainable Development Goals advanced by the United Nations as a basis for the construction of a video depicting what they wanted to accomplish in order to shape a better world. The freedom for Lions Clubs to select the contests they wanted to support enabled them to reach out and collaborate with school teachers and administrators, local artists and photographers, and media specialists to assist with the technical production and support of these initiatives.

These community-based projects and LCI contest initiatives appealed to Lions Clubs because they provided hands-on opportunities for service. But, with the support of grants from LCIF, Lions Clubs could do much more.

LCIF-supported Projects

Because LCIF's purpose has been to provide support for Lions Clubs worldwide to serve their local and global community through grants, the establishment of priorities for how to distribute the grant funds was essential. As this phase of collaborative expansion continued, LCIF prioritized four areas supporting key aspects of service offered by Lions Clubs: Saving sight; providing disaster relief; supporting youth; and meeting humanitarian needs. As of 2017, LCIF distributed more than US $1 billion in grants to support service in these areas around the world

(LCIF, 2017, p. 356). Figure 2.1 provides a breakdown in US dollars by major category.

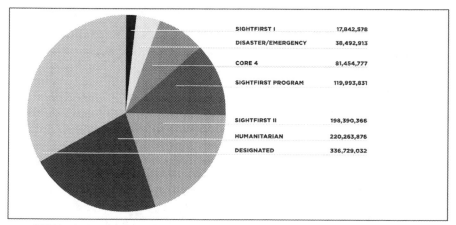

SIGHTFIRST I	17,842,578
DISASTER/EMERGENCY	38,492,913
CORE 4	81,454,777
SIGHTFIRST PROGRAM	119,993,831
SIGHTFIRST II	198,390,366
HUMANITARIAN	220,263,876
DESIGNATED	336,729,032

FIGURE 2.1. GRANT FUNDING ALLOCATED BY LCIF BETWEEN 1/1/1970 AND 6/12/201

*Reported grant data categories combined: Disaster/Emergency (catastrophic, emergency); Humanitarian (humanitarian, international assistance, major international service, seed, standard grant, undetermined).

During this stage, LCIF provided five types of grants: Standard grants; Core 4 grants; international assistance grants; disaster grants; and SightFirst grants. In actuality, thousands of grants to support different kinds of service projects were distributed to Lions Clubs in order to provide services to those in need. Perhaps best known were the disaster grants, issued in the form of emergency grants to relieve the immediate needs of a community, major catastrophe grants for long-term rebuilding after a catastrophic disaster, and disaster preparedness grants for preparation, response, and recovery efforts following a natural disaster.

In addition to these disaster grants, standard grants supported large-scale Lions service projects, such as building playgrounds for disabled children, funding vision screening devices, and constructing and expanding schools to provide more educational opportunities. Through Core 4 grants, special initiatives were funded, including Lions Quest, a collaborative project between LCI and local schools. Lions Quest is a life-skills program that teaches young people important character-developing skills, such as social and emotional learning, responsible decision-making, and service learning. International assistance grants supported projects involving two countries whereby a Lions Club in a developed country partnered with a Lions Club in a developing country to provide water wells, medical missions, and eyeglass recycling, to name a few.

The final funding category provided SightFirst grants. Campaign SightFirst I and Campaign SightFirst II were two major fundraising campaigns conducted by LCIF early in the renewal phase focusing on raising money to save sight. Campaign SightFirst I began in 1991 and by 1994, 140+ million US dollars were raised, exceeding the initial goal of 130 million US dollars. Campaign SightFirst II raised an additional sixty-five-plus million US dollars. Grants from these campaigns were awarded to help Lions Clubs fight preventable and reversible blindness, and included projects to build hospitals and clinics, train doctors, distribute medicine, and raise awareness of eye disease. Additional projects stemming from SightFirst I and II received funding designated as SightFirst Program in Figure 2.1.

Funds raised in these campaigns mobilized support for volunteers who transported patients and donor recipients to clinics to receive their surgeries, increased personal giving, and gave of their time to support increased cataract surgeries around the world. LCIF collaborated with the International Agency for the Prevention of Blindness, the World Health Organization, the United Nations, and the Carter Center to combat diabetic retinopathy, trachoma, and river blindness. Following Campaign SightFirst II, river blindness was eliminated in Latin America and several African nations. These collaborative efforts on the prevention and treatment blindness produced major impacts.

Service Platforms

The emergence of service platforms as a way to establish collaborative projects in Lionism is the most recent focus for LCI. Service platforms provide general categories for Lions Clubs and comprise a guide for identifying and carrying out service projects. In fact, the platforms established in LCI Forward as the main areas of focus for the second century of Lionism actually were drawn from what Lions Clubs had been doing for much of the first century: Sharing the vision; engaging youth; relieving hunger; and protecting the environment. Additionally, in 2016, the International Board of Directors approved diabetes and pediatric cancer as future platforms for service. They also undergirded the entire range of platforms with a directive that youth engagement should be part of every platform.

What these platforms accomplished was to open wide the doors for all kinds of projects to serve the particular needs of local communities, as well as to provide opportunities for collaboration with other clubs to have a greater impact globally. For example, a Lions Club could collect and recycle eyeglasses or conduct vision screenings with other clubs to participate on the vision platform; send a young person on an international youth exchange or support a Leo Club on the youth platform; collaborate with other clubs to serve a meal to the homeless or provide access to a community garden giving healthy food for vulnerable people to meet the hunger need; and plant trees to make the community a healthier place to live as a way to participate on the environment platform.

To encourage collaboration, LCI promoted Worldwide Weeks of Service in order for local clubs to partner with other service organizations or businesses. These Weeks of Service followed an established pattern with Worldwide Week of Service in Sight occurring in October; Worldwide Week of Service to Fight Hunger in January; and Worldwide Week of Service to Protect our Planet scheduled in April. At the time of this publication, over two-thirds of the Lions Clubs around the world reported participating in the Centennial Service Platforms, as reported in Table 2.3. Figures in the table represent a variety of Lions' projects with a range of people benefitted over a four-year period from 2014-2018.

Table 2.3

Self-Reported Club Involvement in Two or More LCI Centennial Service Platforms[6]

Category	Vision	Youth	Hunger	Environment	Percentage/ Total
Clubs Participating	25,531	31,282	25,234	25,016	32,641 (68%)
People Benefitted	27,268,921	56,032,125	38,952,194	54,616,384	177,238,920

Summary

The last thirty years of Lionism were a time of renewal for the association. Sparked by the introduction of women as full members, Lions Clubs sought ways to collaborate and form partnerships to accomplish more with their service activities. Through local projects and LCI initiatives, Lions Clubs continued their commitment to serve their communities in the areas of vision, youth, health, and the environment. With the growing resources of LCIF, funds were available to enable Lions to accomplish more service in the areas of saving sight, providing disaster relief, supporting youth, and providing for humanitarian needs. At the end of one hundred years of service, Lions Clubs International continued its commitment to renewal, using the service platforms identified in LCI Forward to focus the service activities of Lions Clubs on key areas: vision, youth, hunger; environment, diabetes, and pediatric cancer.

Conclusion

Helen Keller's story was a call to service for a fledgling organization coming into existence in the early years of the twentieth century. As

---

[6] Join the Centennial Service Challenge, 2017.

Lions Clubs International moved through four phases of organizational development, it experienced phases of expansion that changed the association as it evolved. Building the organization through the use of service activities enabled LCI to exist and survive through challenging social, economic, and political periods in history. As the organization became more mature, its leaders promoted service activities as a way to coordinate and collaborate to have a greater impact on local communities and the world. Through it all, the motto, *We Serve!* united Lions around the world, attracting new members and providing stability for clubs to continue their efforts on behalf of those in need.

In his book, *Pillars of Lionism* (1997) Lion G. S. Aweida detailed the leadership years of those who had been president of the association up to that point in its history. Included were the texts of major presidential speeches. The words of Judge Brian Stevenson provide a fitting ending for this chapter about Lions service. Past International President Stevenson stressed:

> We urge you to be proud of Lions Clubs International—to be proud of our history—to be proud of our traditions—to be proud of our present—and of our dreams for the future. In twelve months, when our stewardship is over, let there be no doubt throughout the world community as to the meaning behind these two inspirational—profound—and all-inclusive words: *Me Palvelemme; Nous Servons; Wir Dienen; Noi Serviamo; Ti Tjana; Nosotros Servimos; Nos Servimos; Wareware Wa Hoshi Suru; Urinen Pong Sah Han Tah; Wo Men Fu Wu; We Serve.* (p. 914)

While service was the core premise behind the creation of Lions Clubs International, the question remains: What motivated its members to join and serve those in need? Chapter 3 provides some insight about the cultural determinants of service and what motivates people to serve.

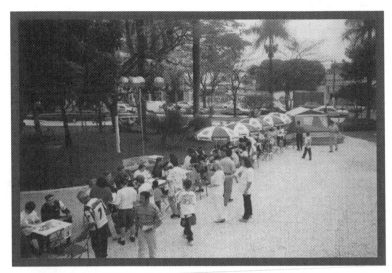

Groups at tables, Lions Club at Leme Health Fair, Brazil

Lions Club built shelters in India 1940-1960

Chapter 3

The Call to Service

"We are all part of this society that is constantly evolving. By doing different things that change the life of someone else, the community, and later the whole country, we help to make the world a better place." (10:16)

In chapter 2, a thematic history of Lions Clubs International revealed the deeply-rooted commitment to service that formed the bedrock for Lions around the world as they responded to the needs of people and their communities. These acts of service changed lives and came at no small price in terms of time, financial support, and personal commitment. While no one will dispute the claim that LCI is the world's largest service organization, the question remains: What motivates people to serve with such a deep commitment? In addition, do all people serve for the same reasons?

The topic of volunteerism and what motivates people to serve has grabbed the attention of researchers, CEOs, and non-profit organizations worldwide. They want to answer the question of why people choose to give freely of their time in order to provide services without any monetary gain. Some researchers claim that volunteerism can improve self-esteem since it makes a person feel good to help others; while others suggest that volunteering helps a person overcome social isolation (Elrod, 2013). This chapter begins with the story of the founding members representing various business men's clubs as they came together to forge the initial agreement to affiliate. Then, an exploration of cultural characteristics is offered to explain how motivation and volunteerism are understood in different regions of the world. Finally, the findings of the survey data reveal six reasons that Lions shared about what first motivated them to make the decision to serve the needs of others.

The Founders' Story

On June 7, 1917, representatives from The Business Circle of Chicago, the Vortex Clubs of St. Louis and Detroit, the Business and Professional Men's Association of St. Paul, the Optimist Club of Indianapolis, Indiana, and the International Associations of Lions from Evansville, Indiana, met in the East Room of the LaSalle Hotel in Chicago. While they came from different clubs with different organizational cultures, their purpose was to form a unified international organization; and at the center of the meeting was Melvin Jones who corresponded with and invited these men to come together at a noon meeting of The Business Circle.

The meeting was called to order by G. W. Milligan, chairman of the Noon Meetings Committee of The Business Circle. After his initial greeting, Milligan called on Melvin Jones to lead the discussion about forming an international organization. While several issues needed attention, the discussion centered on what such an organization would be named. Because each of the represented organizations already had a name, Jones acknowledged the need for compromise and suggested that The Business Circle would sacrifice its name because—as he suggested—the rose would smell just as sweet by another name (Minutes of Meeting, 1917).

After passing a resolution that the luncheon meeting would constitute a business meeting for the local hosts, a motion was introduced and passed to authorize the Board of Directors of The Business Circle to enter into negotiation with Dr. W. P. Woods of the International Association of Lions Clubs and the other clubs, to become affiliated. Following this action, The Business Circle members adjourned their meeting. Subsequently, F. M. Hallenbeck and Melvin Jones were elected

Chair and Secretary of the joint meeting and each of the visiting clubs was given voting delegate.

Choosing what to name the organization was the focus of discussion. Each of the clubs presented reasons why their cherished names should be selected. Then, Dr. W. P. Woods spoke, suggesting that the name of the organization was not as important as the men behind it. Because he believed that the Lion was a symbol of strength and the King of Beasts, the Lions Club would be the King of all. He concluded: "Gentlemen, I do not believe the name has much to do with the success of an organization, but it is the men behind it. The Lion is a symbol of strength, it is the King of Beasts, and we desire to make the Lions Clubs the KING OF CLUBS" (Minutes of Meeting, 1917).

The chief rival to the International Association of the Lions Clubs was the Optimist Club. But representatives noted that because Optimist Club already was operating in several U. S. cities, the adoption of that name for the international association would mean that if any current or future Lions Club or another business clubs also were operating in those cities, they would have to be disbanded or merged, destroying the purpose of forming an international organization of clubs. At this point, a motion was made by Mr. Kaercher of St. Louis and seconded by D. S. Sattler of The Business Circle: That the representatives in session form an organization of the clubs not now in conflict with one another, details to be worked out, and a national name be adopted later, subject to the ratification by the clubs represented by the voting member (Minutes of Meeting, 1917). The motion was carried, with the Optimists not voting. At this point, Melvin Jones asked for and was granted a recess in order to talk with The Business Circle directors.

When the meeting reconvened, following an expressed interest by The Business Circle in accepting a charter from the International Association of The Lions Clubs, Dr. Woods took the floor and extended the following invitation in the form of a resolution:

> Whereas all clubs represented here today have different names, and whereas The Lions Clubs already have an international organization, with approximately thirty clubs in different parts of the United States, and

whereas The Lions Clubs are not now represented in any other cities represented by the other clubs; therefore, as president of the International Association of Lions Clubs, I hereby extend an invitation to these clubs to accept charters in the International Association of Lions Clubs and become a part and parcel of our organization. If you accept this invitation there will be no membership charged, and all we ask is to adopt our name and pay dues to the International Association, which are at a rate of $1.00 per member, per year, payable semi-annually in advance. (Minutes of Meeting, 1917)

Mr. Sattler of the Chicago Club moved to accept the invitation, subject to the ratification of the different clubs within sixty days and reporting back to the acting secretary, Melvin Jones. The motion carried unanimously with Jones instructed to print copies of the minutes and to send them to the clubs represented, as well as to any other clubs who might be of interest. With this action, the foundation for Lions Clubs International was established.

The Impact of Culture

Why someone would want to join such a club as what emerged from the meeting on June 7, 1917, or volunteer to serve the needs of others has its roots in culture. After all, the cultural perspective of a person shapes how they interact and engage with others. As people, we are not born with culture, we are born into culture. Culture is learned, so when people take on a service perspective, it must come from somewhere.

Larry Sarbaugh (1979), a noted observer and scholar of culture and communication, introduced a way to sort out how people acquire their cultural perspectives. He suggested that our understanding of language, perceptions about relationships with others, willingness to accept different values and behaviors, and worldview reveal a great deal about the kinds of people we are when it comes to interacting with others from our own or different cultural backgrounds.

Language and Perceived Intent

When it comes to providing service to others, the most meaningful language we use is often nonverbal, as words are not needed to express concern or to provide support. After all, a smile or a hug provides reassurance and prompts reciprocation. But the other three perspectives are more intentional in the way they influence how we enter into service and reflect upon our commitment to serve. For example, when a person makes a commitment to volunteer or serve the needs of others, the intent of that action is to be helpful, not hurtful. If a person's intent is to be neutral, that choice may be perceived as hurtful because the needs of others are being neglected or minimized. People who choose to volunteer and engage in service must have a helpful intent if their actions are to be perceived as genuine.

Knowledge and Acceptance

When serving the needs of others, we often are confronted with people having different values and behaviors than our own. In these situations, we must respond in one of four ways. The first option proposes that we will know and accept the values and behaviors of the person to be helped. This perspective often is directed toward people with whom we share a common background or point of view. For example, you may want to support young people from your community. You know the children and accept their proposed school trip as a valuable learning opportunity, so you volunteer to work at a fundraiser to help finance the trip. You know them and accept them as being worthy of your efforts.

Not knowing but being willing to accept the values and behaviors of others is a second orientation. In this case, you are volunteering to help an individual or group that needs your assistance, even though you don't know them. From individual to group, the world is full of people we don't know. Whether in the context of your own community or in a village on the other side of the globe; recognizing the needs of those with vision or hearing impairments or victims of natural disasters like floods, hurricanes, and fires, is worth your action. Volunteers who take on the mantle of service to others without knowing who they serve is the mark of a true servant leader. In this case, you don't know who you may be helping, but you accept the beneficiary as worthy of help.

The final two orientations follow the same comparative way of thinking but are not well-suited to the genuine service perspective. In one of these instances, you know who needs your help, but you do not accept the person as worthy of your service; and in the other, you don't know who you are helping and you are not willing to accept the Other as worthy of your assistance. As an example of this first situation, you may know that there is a worldwide need to support disaster relief following a hurricane somewhere in the world, but you are not willing to accept that helping LCIF to raise funds is more important than supporting your community needs. While both may be important, your commitment to service is conditional, depending upon your acceptance of who deserves your attention. In the last situation, you are unaware of the needs of those around you, and you choose not to get involved. Like an ostrich with its head in the sand, people with this orientation often actually receive more service than they provide.

As these examples illustrate, your knowledge and acceptance of the beliefs and values of others reveals your orientation toward service. In the end, the capacity to be willing to accept the responsibility to serve the needs of others without knowing them personally is the mark of person who is truly committed to the service perspective.

Worldview

The fourth way to look at how people view service is to consider what some call worldview. A person's worldview is shaped by a number of factors, including how you view your life, what you consider to be your reason for living, and how you see yourself in relationship to the universe. You might see your life from a position of privilege, where you have been afforded enough money, prestige, and respect to do what you want, when you want, with whomever you want. In contrast, your life may be one of hardship, where your choices are limited by economic or social factors beyond your personal control. And then, there is everything in between where you confront the benefits and challenges of daily living from your particular place in life.

Depending upon how you view your life, your reasons for living may vary. Often this variance has something to do with how you look at the concept of time. Some people live to honor the past, holding onto memories and traditions of a past time as a way to create stability and purpose in their lives. Others live in the present, needing to make sure they have enough time to eat and a place to sleep without being able to think to any great extent about what the future will hold. Then, there are those who plan for the future, making choices today that may benefit them at some time in the future.

Considering your view of life and reason for living, your relationship with the universe may be one of control, subjugation, or coexistence. If you are fortunate to have control over the resources you need to live and are able to take steps to plan for your future, you have a worldview of action. For example, when you see a problem, you are proactive. The costs or resources needed to solve the problem do not stop you. You become a servant leader as you use your power and find a way to serve individually or with others to achieve the goals you seek.

In the second case, subjugation means being under the control of some other group or force. Many people are subjugated to nature and are unable to change the natural patterns that control them. Others may be enslaved by drug usage or physical dependency and are unlikely to provide genuine service to others while under the influence.

When coexistence is your worldview, people cope with the particular circumstances that face them. They are able to take some action, but do so only as a reaction to what has happened to them. They have the ability to do something to take care of themselves, but they do not assert their capacity to exert control over the situation to take care of others.

In summary, the cultural perspectives people learn provide the foundation for their service orientation. By understanding our own perspectives, we shape the kind of volunteer we strive to become. Learning to communicate with care and compassion will build positive relationships. Offering a helpful approach when providing support for those in need of assistance will foster friendships and acceptance. Being willing to serve the needs of people who may be unknown to you but for whom you are willing to accept as worthy of your effort is the mark of a true servant. Finally, having the resources and perspective—individually or collaboratively—to affect the lives of those in need should be the goal of those who are called to service. In reality, these cultural characteristics shape the persona of volunteerism.

A Look at Cultural Perspectives

This general orientation to culture provides us with a way to characterize people who are committed to serving the needs of others. Service takes many forms around the world. What is considered to be prominent in one area or country might be less relevant in other regions of the world. In an effort to learn more about how volunteering and caring for others is perceived in different parts of the world, scholars have conducted studies—some anecdotal, others more generalizable—to help us to identify and understand cultural differences.

In the following discussion, the findings from some of these studies illustrate how service and volunteerism are viewed in different parts of the world. These studies conducted by academic scholars should not be viewed as making broad claims about what all people from the identified areas believe or how they act. Rather, these studies show the range of issues and circumstances that may provide the basis for motivating people to serve the needs of others. While not meant to be exhaustive, this brief examination provides a look at the variety of ways service and volunteerism have been studied and discussed around the world.

Studies Involving African Cultures

Over the years, studies have been conducted to identify volunteerism and service activities in Africa. One such study identified the motivation for volunteering in South Africa. Swartz and Colvin (2015) followed community health workers serving in economically depressed areas of that country. Their findings revealed four factors affecting the motivation to serve: gender, Ubuntu, religious background, and economics. Women were found to be more inclined to volunteer because of their frequently assigned cultural roles as being the caregivers. From this role, they often experienced an emotional toll resulting from working with terminally-ill HIV/AIDS patients. Most African volunteers believed that without their presence helping the sick, no one else would do so. Swartz and Colvin also found that many of the participants reported that they continued to volunteer because of their moral obligation to the community and to sustain their communities' religious and economic structures.

A common thread that is woven throughout these studies about African volunteerism is Ubuntu, also known as "African-ness" or ethics. The idea of Ubuntu maintains an inherent *ethic of care* in Africans, as well as an interconnectedness and sense of responsibility for each other (Serwah, 2011). Ubuntu is considered as a social value that defies prejudice and xenophobia, shaping healthy and productive social relationships (John, 2015). Thus, Ubunto is an all-encompassing term used in many African countries to describe and identify sustained volunteerism as highly ethical behavior. While the variety of ethnic and cultural groups in Africa makes it impossible to generalize about why all Africans volunteer, Ubunto helps to explain the basis for why many Africans are called to service.

Studies Involving Asian Cultures

Similar to the difficulties associated with describing an all-African approach to service, studies about volunteerism in Asian cultures are equally scarce. This makes the drawing of conclusions difficult. However, among the studies conducted about volunteerism in Asian cultures, hard work and careful planning generally characterized how people viewed the nature and purpose of life.

Since Asians' familial roles are inherently ingrained in who they are, a study by Warburton and Winteron in 2010 concluded that finding a new role after retirement, where they felt needed and respected, was vital for Asian people. Asians in the study also reported that time banks were viewed as a main reason for volunteering. Basically, using the time bank means they volunteer in the present—while they are physically able—in hopes that one day, they will benefit from the service of people who will take care of them. One volunteer described the importance of his plan to store up good will as his biggest hope for the future.

In some studies, positive and successful aging was found to be chief among the motivations behind sustained volunteerism among Asian people. Successful aging consists of being healthy, contributing to the community, and maintaining close relations with friends and family (Chen, 2015; Chong, Rochelle, & Liu, 2013). By volunteering, Asians are able to fulfill their societal concerns and experience a smoother transition to old age through sustained contributions to the community. This study's focus on successful aging reflects a self-directed motivation for volunteering.

Studies Involving Latin American Cultures

Very little research has been undertaken about volunteerism in Latin American cultures. However, commonly identified reasons for volunteering have included attachment to needs in an affected area, a sense of national unity to solve problems, and the need to respond in the absence of adequate governmental responses following a disaster (Brzozowski, 2013; Guy, 2009). According to studies conducted in different Latin American communities, volunteers are very committed to helping people in areas affected by natural disasters. Nationalism is another reason for increased service to meet the needs of a particular area or group of citizens. Finally, lack of governmental action to provide for the needs of the poor was cited as a motivation for individual service. Juan Carr, founder of the Solidarity Network, believed inadequate government action was a major reason prompting volunteerism:

> Ten years ago, we still left it up to the leaders to do things, but now we Argentines have realized that the leaders don't do anything for us. We went from a period of indifference to a period of emotional solidarity.

Solidarity, or people working together to provide services to meet local community needs, provides motivation for service.

Studies Involving European Cultures

Scholars have been describing European cultures for centuries, but few studies have explored the cultural differences of volunteers. Presently, when addressing the needs of refugees from the war-torn Middle East entering different countries across Europe, one study found that Northern Europeans (Germans and the Dutch) were perceived to be more likely to volunteer than southern Europeans (Dieckmann, Grimm, Unfried, Utikal, & Valmasoni, 2016). This perception may be the basis for the claims by some critics that southern Europeans have done less to assist refugees because they have assumed the northern Europeans would do it.

On an individual level, research has suggested that Europeans who experience high stress and low reward jobs during their midlife are less likely to volunteer after retirement (Wahrendorf, Blane, Matthews, & Siegrist, 2016). Some suggest this results because of the perception that volunteering will be similar to working. If working resulted in few rewards, volunteering was likely to be similarly unrewarding.

A few studies investigated the influence of religious background on volunteerism in Europe, reaching different conclusions. Ruiter and Degraff (2006) found that being in a faith community was correlated positively with volunteerism, as the activities associated with service reflected adherence to scripture; while Prouteau and Sardinha (2015) and Lim and MacGregor (2012) found that when compared to secular countries, religious affiliation actually had a negative impact on volunteerism because people focused their energy on activities associated with their church, rather than serving community needs. These conflicting findings suggest that further research should be done to understand this relationship; and they underscore that when it comes to culture, drawing conclusions is difficult due to the many factors that can influence why a person participates in service-related activities.

Studies Involving North American Cultures

Research on volunteers in North America has shown that people choose to volunteer for activities that reflect their personal values and identity (Clary, Snyder, Ridge, Copeland, Stukas, Haugen, & Miene,

1998). People who believe in maintaining a beautiful community likely will volunteer to clean up the park; or people who want to make sure that vision problems are detected early in life will join a vision-screening team. Similarly, different people can engage in the same volunteer activity for completely different reasons if they believe the cause is worth supporting (Finkelstien, 2009).

Some studies suggest that people volunteer so they will be noticed by others as doing something worthwhile (Bidee, Vantilgorgh, Pepermans, Huybrechts, Willems, Jegers, & Hofmas, 2013; Brunell, Tumblin, Buelow, 2014; Weinstein, 2010). Other studies show that working together as a group is more important than receiving individual recognition. These differing perspectives may be a result of the tension for North Americas between being individuals and being part of a collective or group.

Current research also suggests that women volunteer in different organizations and for different projects based upon the level of empowerment they feel. Some women choose to volunteer in the nonprofit sector because they feel empowered to work for a worthy cause. Other research claims that women volunteer in the nonprofit sector as a result of feeling less empowered in the private sector (Themudo, 2009). Volunteerism also can depend heavily upon whether a person feels homogenous with, or fits easily into the group participating in the activity (Lipford & Yandle, 2009).

Finally, researchers believe that if volunteers have extrinsic motivations such as improving social status or career advancement, they are more likely to experience a faster burnout rate than volunteers with intrinsic motivation, such as feelings of satisfaction or a sense of fulfillment. The personal value of giving of oneself for a worthy cause can sustain a long-term commitment to volunteerism (Moreno-Jiminez & Villodres, 2019).

In Short

Culture shapes the way people view volunteering and service to others. The stories of volunteers reveal that showing compassion and support through expressions and actions shows a genuinely helpful intent toward those in need. Those who are willing to serve the needs of people they do not know, and are able to take action—either individually or collaboratively—to help are role models with a true volunteer spirit. But the question remains: What reasons do these role models of service provide for why they decided to start volunteering in their communities?

What the Survey Revealed about Motivation for Service

The findings from the survey revealed six main themes describing the reasons why people made the commitment to serve the needs of others.[7] These themes were drawn from 743 total responses to the question: What was your initial reason for volunteering to serve the needs of others? These themes include: It's part of my personal identity; it's my heritage; I want to be socially connected with other like-minded people; I experience personal development and satisfaction; my service makes others feel better; my service makes the world a better place; and other reasons.

Figure 3.1 provides a look at how the themes were represented among the respondents. Selected responses for each of the themes are provided to help establish a profile of why people were motivated to volunteer or provide service to others.

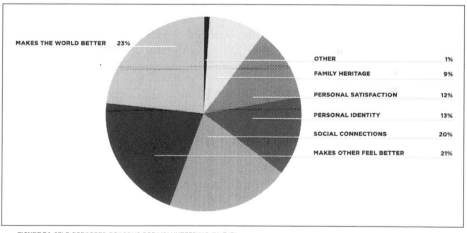

FIGURE 3.1. SELF-REPORTED REASONS FOR VOLUNTEERING (N=743)

---

[7] There were six responses that did not fit into one of the six themes identified here. These comments were either unclear, unrelated, or the respondent indicated that they didn't remember why they started serving. For these reasons, they have been excluded.

Personal Identity

Among the 743 responses to this question, ninety-five participants indicated they were motivated to serve the needs of others because it was part of their personal identity to do so. Some indicated that they were born to serve: "[Service] is born from the heart. It's a very pure feeling and I do it not wanting anything in return" (10:54); "helping the others has always been a lifestyle for me" (3:47); and "I was 'born to do that'" (8:61). In other words, service was viewed as an inherent part of who they believe they are: "It was inherent in my nature" (5:81); "I think it's in my character and in my early life experiences as a child having a great curiosity and an interest in other people" (5:95); "the intention [to serve] was natural" (8:18); "I always had this natural inclination to help others" (8:35); and "the instinct to help" (10:92). Whether it is truly inborn or not, the belief that service is part of their being was perceived as a significant reason why they chose to volunteer.

The commitment to service was also viewed as personal, intangible qualities. Among these qualities were desire, love, empathy, and compassion. Many participants identified their attraction to service as desire. For example, "I have a desire to help ..." was commonly referenced with the recipients being described as vulnerable groups, those in a weaker condition, the needy, the poor, or the elderly to name a few. Others considered service to be a function of their loving nature: "My motivation is human. Since I was a child, I have always loved supporting others" (3:45); and "I love to help" (1:6). Having empathy and compassion provided another reason people found themselves motivated to serve: "[My] interest for the Other in general, and a 'natural' empathy" (3:67); and "compassion towards those who are suffering" (5:37, 8:16).

Family Heritage

A second reason identified as the motivation for a commitment to service was family heritage, including family history and religious background. Many respondents identified their parents and family as role models. For instance: "The example was given daily in the actions of my family" (10:96); "My parents educated me in serving people, as they were involved themselves in service since I opened my eyes" (3:6); "Growing up, I followed my father who was a member of Lions Club" (6:29); "I am following my dad's legacy" (8:26); and "an example from my mother, even though she was poor she would help through the church and through Lionism" (10:56). Teachers provided another form of role model for some: "One of my teachers was a Lion and helped me" (10:40).

Religious background also provided a motivation for people to serve, as was noted: "I started with my youth training in the parish" (5:25); "I grew up in a region where volunteer service was a reason to live. I entered the club when I was in school. I served as a staff member at a local church" (10:48); and "As a Christian I was brought up with the idea to help others, and in particular people with less money and or had a health need" (11:25). No matter what the influence for these respondents, their upbringing guided them to service: "I was brought up to help others. Once volunteering on a regular basis, it was the camaraderie that made it worth working at" (11:40).

Social Connections

For twenty percent of the respondents, their motivation for service was related to their friendships and need and desire for social connectedness to others. Friends are powerful motivators for service, as they were mentioned most frequently among the 152 respondents as one of the reasons why they became Lions and began volunteering in their communities. For example: "A good friend of mine asked me if I wanted to join Lions, and told me what they did" (9:32); "I did not really know anything about Lions activities, but a good friend asked me to come along ..." (2:8); "Good friends were part of it, which pulled me along" (2:33); "I became involved with a group of friends, Lions, and I felt I should give my time and my experience to start working in favor of the less fortunate" (5:70); and "A friend of mine got me to start volunteering. I met many nice people volunteering ..." (9:71)

For others, service fulfilled a need for social contact. Specifically, service became a way to extend beyond the home: "I was a stay-at-home mother and wanted to get some counterbalance to housework ... with some time, I was establishing a women's club for the district" (2:21). For others, service was a way to become part of a larger group of people sharing the same outlook: "I want to get involved with many people for the long term" (6:21); and "fraternity, friendship, sharing ideas and the philosophy of serving others" (8:49). One respondent made it quite clear: "I needed friends and joined the Lions" (11:32).

Personal Development and Satisfaction

Some respondents provided personal development and satisfaction as key reasons motivating them to serve. These aspects of service ranged from feeling happy to finding fulfillment and self-worth. Finding personal happiness through service was often mentioned: "From the bottom of my heart, I love doing things that could make me deeply happy" (1:2); "[Service] makes me feel good" (8:83); "It makes me happy knowing that someone else is happy receiving my help" (10:14); and "[Service is a] selfish need; if I can help someone, it makes ME feel good" (11:9)

Service was viewed as providing personal satisfaction and self-worth, especially for those who were retired or had time to spend helping others: "I'm satisfied being able to give relief from suffering to people who for various reasons are in trouble" (5:84); "People in Sweden are raised to do voluntary work ... It always feels good to help other people that need it. It makes me happy and proud" (5:36); "helping, feeling useful, and having the satisfaction to succeed in making someone sad smile" (3:13); and "I'm retired. Need to do something worthwhile ... was widowed, children grown, so had my own time to use productively" (11:33). For some, it was quite simple: "After serving others, I feel I have value" (1:7).

In addition to personal satisfaction, some identified service as giving meaning to life. One of the respondents described this personal development in the following way:

> I started to be aware of the human community when
> I was twelve, at the time when I was a Scout. The Scout
> prayer is: "... teach us how to be generous, to give without
> counting, to fight without begin afraid of the wounds, to
> work without searching for rest, and to give all of ourselves

searching for no reward but the fact of knowing that we are acting according to your mere will." Being useful to others, it is engagement that gives a meaning to my life. (3:62)

Similarly, "we all need each other and helping others gives the tranquility to one's conscience that promotes a happy life ... [Service] fills my spirit with peace and my days are calm with the tranquility of the spirit of doing it" (10:31).

Making Others Feel Better

When the respondents shared their commitment to service because of the desire to make others feel better, the Others they referenced comprised many identities, including: Poorer people; those with abnormalities; those many characterized as the *less fortunate* because of deficiencies in something they needed to enjoy a particular quality of life; the disadvantaged; disabled people; the homeless; and people in need. The clear motivation for most of the 156 people responding in this category was lifting up the spirits or physical conditions of individuals or groups who needed assistance, being present to "release their misery, loneliness" (3:10). One group often mentioned were the lonely and elderly: "So many lonely people, especially the elderly, need closeness and friends" (2:30).

Being able to improve the quality of life provided motivation for many: "I try to help others to increase their life quality; even just a little bit. Whoever receives is really grateful and that's what really matters" (8:29). Witnessing suffering brought some response from volunteers who wanted "to help people that I see suffering and of whom I thought that with a little support or help, there could be change" (10:3). Through it all, the motive remained: "to give some of my time to better the quality of life for those with less so I can return something that my community has done for me" (10:16).

The reality of service for those seeking to make others feel better often is not viewed as excessive by the volunteer who, "Sees that by donating a little bit of my time and money, it's possible to help families in need. This little bit of help is enough to give them hope and dignity" (8:88). Many agreed with the sentiment about this motivation for service: "To help other people that are in need and to be part of an organization known for helping those in need. The uplifting of spirits was amazing when donating/giving food parcels" (11:72).

Make the World a Better Place

The sixth theme describing why people serve the needs of others emerged from their desire to make the world a better place. The 172 people who made this their motivation for service provided a wide range of examples of how making the world better might be accomplished. A very common example focused on helping their own communities: "I want to give back to the community what it gave me: Trust, support and a chance" (4:34); "I want to give back to the community" (1:3); "the initial reason for being a volunteer … was seeing the need in my community for assistance to many people who were ignored by government decisions" (11:13); and "I wanted to give back to my community and our town is a small rural farming community and the Lions were the only service organization in the area" (11:20).

Other volunteers expanded their view to include their regions and countries where political and economic issues needed to be addressed. For example: "I care about the needs of our communities, where disinformation to human rights and disorganization of the people, leads them to inequality" (8:52); and "the urgent need of my country; poverty is bad and volunteering could help mitigate" (10:26). The concern about broader, societal issues prompted many to profess their desire to contribute to the greater good of all: "I wanted to give something back to the society. I am a child of an immigrant family and people helped us a lot, too" (4:1); "Everyone has the right to live equally and sometimes in your life, you might plunge into an abyss. When people are having difficult times, I will give a hand to help and I think that it is the human society's spirit" (6:27); "to give it back to the society in the spirit of solidarity" (8:94); "my biggest motivation is without a doubt to better society that has a low respect of value, to make the society that I and my future children will live in better is without a doubt the most important cause" (10:10);

As a final dimension of the responses about making the world a better place, people became more philosophical in their remarks: "We need to give in order to receive, and if we give love we receive love. This is how we will succeed in changing the world in a positive and permanent way" (3:12); "reducing the inequalities which are very often temporary in the life of a human or a family. Lowering the inequalities reduces bitterness and social and administrative violence" (3:33); "I wish to serve and collaborate for a better and happier world" (8:2); and "the world needs more people to care for each other" (9:56). It was in this area where the theme of joining with others in Lions Clubs to provide their service reflected what one person described as: "channeling the power through an institution with global recognition and respect; providing solidarity through acts of service help those in need" (10:43).

Summary

The six themes reflected in the responses of the participants provide a range of motivations for why people make a commitment to serve the needs of others. For those who were motivated because of their personal identity, examples described aspects of their individual personalities and intangible qualities, such as love, empathy, and compassion. The role of family heritage and background was a second theme, with parents and teachers, as well as religious convictions playing a major role in leading them to a life of service. For those seeking social connections, the invitation from and involvement of friends played a key role in motivating the respondents to begin serving the needs of others. The fourth theme focusing on personal development and satisfaction was supported by examples of how service provided volunteers with positive feelings about themselves, and about giving meaning to their lives. Motivation to improve the lives of others was another reason for volunteering, with the identification of specific groups—the poor, the elderly, and people in need—as compelling. Making a difference in the quality of life for others was essential to their service. Finally, the theme of making the world a better place represented the largest percentage of responses. Having a desire to help their communities, countries, society, and the world at large motivated people to begin volunteering and joining Lions Clubs as a way to work together for the common good.

Conclusion

Chapter 3 revealed six major themes that categorized what motivated people to make a commitment to serve the needs of others. Not all people choose to serve for the same reasons, due to the impact of different languages, perceptions of intent, acceptance of beliefs and values, and worldviews. However, despite cultural differences, overarching reasons associated with personal identity, family heritage, social connections, personal satisfaction and development, desire to improve communities, and desire to make the world a better place motivated people to take up the role of the volunteer to serve to those in need. With this in mind, chapter 4 will explore the reasons that sustain the commitment to service as a lifelong goal.

Chapter 4

Calling Others to Serve

"Everyone is unique. You have to find their ON button and craft your words to fit them. Community service, helping the blind, leader dog, and Hadley are all tools to use, but local events that they can take part in and feel part of, work the best for me." (11:37)

When attempting to motivate someone to take some action voluntarily, it is necessary to find the right message or approach; in other words, find their *"on"* button. Some people need to have all of the facts before they will make a commitment; others need to feel the emotion associated with the situation before they will take action. In order to be successful, the motivator needs to understand the different variables affecting how the call to service may be perceived. Chapter 3 explored the cultural aspects of service. From this perspective, the highest level of service came from those who could communicate with or without language, had a helpful intent when they served, gave of themselves without knowing the recipients of their assistance, and had a world view reflecting a commitment to take action and not be stopped by problems or obstacles in the way of the completion of a project or endeavor. While the world may be filled with hundreds of culturally different groups and perspectives, the cultural perspective of the volunteer—particularly in Lionism—appeared to be universal and found among people from around the world (Curtis, Grabb, & Baer, 1992).

In addition to the impact of culture, six broad themes emerged that encompassed the reasons why people initially accepted the call to service, ranging from physiological to altruistic. These themes provided a wide range of perspectives for why people served, including: Service was part of their personal identity; their willingness to serve was due to family heritage and role models; service connected them with friends and associates in a social and meaningful activity; service enhanced their personal development and satisfaction; providing service made those in need feel better; and service to others made the world a better place in which to live. Within these themes, the individual responses were as varied as the people who offered them.

Now in chapter 4, the focus shifts to explore the reasons motivating people to continue their service over time and how their motivation functioned as a way to call others to serve. Specifically, what are the intrinsic and extrinsic motivators that encourage people to continue their service activities? And, how are these motivators reflected in the reasons used to recruit others to accept the call to serve? Let's begin with the story of Lions Clubs International's founder Melvin Jones and those aspects of service that motivated him to sustain his lifetime commitment to the association. Then, we can explore the extant research revealing personal motivations for serving those in need, with particular emphasis on how that motivation is sustained over time. This analysis is followed by survey findings from Lions around the world, revealing the role of service as an intrinsic motivator. Additionally, the reasons used to encourage others to serve provide insight into why volunteers have sustained their commitment over extended periods of time. The chapter concludes with implications for service organizations as they encourage individuals to accept the call to service.

Melvin's Story

In a book of stories explaining why people choose to serve the needs of others, the inclusion of one such story told by the Founder of LCI—Melvin Jones—seems obvious. In fact, due to his role as a Founder and servant leader for over half of his life, selecting the right story, or one that meant something to him, posed a challenge for someone like the author who first joined a Lions Club over two decades after Jones' death. I never had the opportunity to meet Melvin Jones, but his influence has been shared with me on numerous occasions through stories told by others, some who actually knew and worked with him. It is unnecessary to provide a biography of this man because others have provided rich histories of his role in starting the association (see Casey & Douglas, 1949; daSilva, 2014; Kleinfelder & Brennan, *n.d.*; Martin, 1991; Martin & Kleinfelder, 2008). But, for the benefit of those reading this book, allow me to share a perspective on Melvin Jones that may shed some light on why he sustained his commitment to the dream of lifting up through the work of Lions Clubs International all those who needed a helping hand.

While LCI was founded in 1917, the seed for this organization was planted in March 1913, when Melvin Jones was invited by William Towne of The Business Circle to lunch at the Boston Oyster House to meet some of the members (Casey & Douglas, 1949). In 1909, membership in The Business Circle was around 200 men; but when Melvin came to lunch, membership had dropped to around thirty-nine. He noted that there were only seventeen present the day he was introduced to the idea of joining a community group. His first thought was to ask why such groups couldn't do something to help improve their communities. For anyone interested in joining what would later be known as a service club, there simply wasn't any such thing before 1917. In fact, in the early twentieth century, community clubs existed for the benefit of themselves, rather than for people who were not members. While creating organizations was not uncommon in the United States during the Progressive Era, when people formed local clubs and groups, they reflected the interests of those who started them. For those organizations that drew people from the business community, the philosophy of you scratch my back, I'll scratch yours, prevailed as bankers, venture capitalists, politicians, and insurance brokers to name a few, joined with the goal to expand their contacts and fuel their enterprises.

Into this environment came Melvin Jones, whom observers noted, "... was probably the last man in the world anybody would have picked out as a crusader, reformer, uplifter, or organizer" (Casey & Douglas, 1949, p. 3). But, associates and colleagues would later note: "He was gregarious. He liked people. He made friends easily and kept them" (p. 4). These personal qualities and his focus on developing lasting relationships emerged and functioned as his motivation for expanding membership beyond his immediate geographical area to form and sustain an international association.

How Melvin Jones became the person he was most certainly can be attributed to his family history. Born January 13, 1880, in Fort Thomas, Arizona, he spent his youth following his father and family on a path that ultimately led him to Chicago. In his twenties, he joined Johnson & Higgins, insurance brokers; and by 1913, he ambitiously was the head of his own agency. His success was attributed to his personality and unique ability to find out and understand what motivated people to believe or act the way they did. According to some, "he had a talent for finagling ... or diplomacy ... membership was another form of salesmanship; providing something that somebody needs" (Casey & Douglas, 1949, p. 6). These talents would serve him well and through a service organization, Melvin Jones found the way to meet the growing needs in the world of his day.

Because he was willing to speak up, the elders in The Business Circle decided that he should be called upon to take on more leadership, so they elected him as secretary January 1, 1914 (Casey and Douglas, 1949, p. 7). But instead of just maintaining the records, he began inviting his friends and acquaintances to join what was now called The Circle. A new energy emerged as Melvin encouraged potential members to join with a group whose purpose was not self-serving but designed to do something for someone else. According to Jones, "any association that presumes to leadership in the community will have to offer something more than business reciprocity among the members" (Casey & Douglas, 1949, p. 20).

This was a revolutionary concept at the time, and one hundred years later, we know its message continues to resonate with people around the world. He successfully recruited more and more members, making room for people from all professions to join in meaningful service. His home became the office for The Circle and he spent long hours corresponding with like-minded people across the country. He visited other clubs and organizations, noting the qualities and best practices that could be incorporated into a larger entity.

His wife helped him tremendously, but often stated that he was working himself to death for others without being paid. He then said, "I'm finding out ... that you don't get very far until you start doing something for somebody else. And I'm beginning to believe it might help some of these clubs, like The Circle, to take that to heart" (Casey & Douglas, 1949, p. 9). This became known as Jones' Law.

Melvin Jones was perhaps thirty-seven years old when his part time labors on behalf of The Business Circle pushed the insurance business out of his office. As Lion historians would later describe, "Jones recognized his métier at once and never looked back" (Casey & Douglas, 1949, p. 16). For Jones, Lions Clubs International functioned as a vehicle for building and sharing the joy of lasting friendships, comradery, and service to others. Late in life, he shared the following story that revealed his unique perspective on the value of a global association:

> In one of the suburbs of Chicago I own … a strip of land of approximately four acres. One rather warm Sunday I strolled out to look things over. I saw two garter snakes sunning themselves. They thought they owned the place. I left them and went on to a ground squirrel that chattered defiantly in an attempt to drive me away from his place.
>
> As I came to the birdhouses I found that the bluebirds and the sparrows were having it out over the right to a bird box. They, too, owned the place. Then the bees disputed the rights of ownership of the flowers. My wife, who says she owns the place herself, told me to get rid of them. But if you want to know who really owns the place, just come prowling around and let our dog see you. Yes, the dog, the birds, the bees, all claim ownership of my home.
>
> It is wintertime now. There are no bees, no flowers, no birds. So, I raise my sad eyes to the direction of the southern wind, and say, "Hurry, hurry, southern breeze; bring back spring; bring back summer; bring back the flowers, the bees, the birds, my wife, my dog, and say to them that the place I thought was mine is theirs, too. It is our home."

Now who owns this club—Tom? Jim? Frank? John? John likes to shake hands with everyone. Tom likes to sing. Harry likes to propose resolutions. Jim likes to be toastmaster. Frank likes to do the highbrow stuff. It's their club. I like to sit back and feel that I own the club too. So, my club is their club and their club is my club and all together it is our club. And our club belongs to the community just as much as it belongs to us. I have often said that the Lions Club is a corporation of friends and has for its capital stock "friendship." Every member in a Lions Club is a friend of every other member, and as the members of a club are linked together, so, also, are the clubs linked together in the Association. From another point of view, every member in a club is a partner of every other member.

So, there are approximately 400,000 partners in this great Association of friends. Members of the Association place a very high value on friendship. As a friend, I serve you. You, knowing that I am your friend, accept my service. There is a great deal of practical wisdom in old Omar Khayyam. And one of his observations will be with me till the day I die. "He who has a thousand friends has not a friend to spare." No one could express more beautifully the reason for our being ... We are primarily friends, friends to our Club, friends to our Association, friends to one another—and yet not one to spare. (Casey & Douglas, 1949, pp. 240—244)

As an observer, one compelling message drawn from Melvin's story suggests that in an organization of friends where service is rendered to help those in need, every member's contribution is needed. Melvin Jones devoted his life to the encouragement of others to accept this call to service.

Theoretical Underpinnings

Scholars and practitioners have learned a great deal about what motivates an individual to act or respond in a particular way. Specifically, this chapter focuses on why people volunteer, how service fulfills a function for those who volunteer, the factors that motivate a person to sustain a commitment to service over an extended period of time, and how matching the motivation for service with how volunteering functions is essential in the recruitment of others.

Why People Volunteer

The process of volunteering begins with a personal decision to participate in a project or activity that provides service to others. Psychologists E. Gil Clary and Mark Snyder noted:

> Volunteering is marked by several key characteristics: the helper must seek out the opportunity to help, the helper arrives at this decision after a period of deliberation, the helper provides assistance over time, and the helper's decisions about beginning to help and continuing to help are influenced by whether the particular activity fits with the helper's own needs and goals. (1999, p. 156)

When the act of volunteering reinforces the helper's needs and goals, it functions as a motivator for service.

The functional approach to motivation has its roots in psychology and suggests that when people engage in voluntary service, the same act of service may serve entirely different psychological functions for different people. In other words, engagement in a service project may reflect different motivations for the participants. For example, volunteering at a vision screening center may fulfill a value function for one individual (e.g., vision screening is important for children), a career function for another volunteer (e.g., helping children will look good on my resume), and a social function a third volunteer (e.g., this is a good chance for me to spend times with my friends). All three functions represent valid reasons for service and suggest different motives for volunteering. The functional approach to motivation was clearly evident from the responses in chapter 3 where people gave different reasons for volunteering.

Motivators for Service

Scholars suggest that people make decisions to sustain their ongoing commitment to service when they realize that what they are doing fulfills the functions most persuasive to them. In other words, the more that service functions in meaningful ways for participants, the more persuaded they will be to continue volunteering. As a way to identify how volunteering functions for different people, Clary and associates (1998) developed the Volunteer Function Inventory (VFI). This psychological measurement scale identified six functions as persuasive for people when determining their motivation for service. These are further explained below and include the following functions: understanding, value, protective, career, social, and enhancement. The researchers found that these six functions were distinct and identifiable across a range of individuals who identified themselves as motivated volunteers.

The understanding function of service provides an opportunity for volunteers to exercise knowledge, skills, and abilities that otherwise might go unpracticed. For example, when a person indicates that, "volunteering allows me to gain a new perspective on things," the act of service functions to increase the volunteer's understanding and ability to interact with other people. When an act of service represents deeply held values, dispositions, and convictions, the value function is fulfilled. Comments like, "I am genuinely concerned about the particular group I am serving," and "I feel compassion toward people in need," function to reinforce values as a motivation for service. For some volunteers, the act of service takes on a protective function, as a defense mechanism buffering against undesirable or threatening truths about the self. For example, when a person reveals that, "doing volunteer work relieves me of some of the guilt over being more fortunate than others," the act of service functions to protect the ego of the volunteer. When volunteers view service as helping them in their chosen professions, the act of service serves a career function. For instance, statements such as: "I can make new contacts that might help my business or career," and "volunteering will look good on my résumé," reveal the career-oriented motivation that service provides. The social function supports the belief that people want to fit in with important reference groups and their friends when engaged in service. Reasons such as, "My friends volunteer," and "volunteering is an important activity to the people I know," demonstrates the importance of engaging in service with one's social network. Finally, when volunteering is described as producing positive feelings that promote the ego's growth and development, the act of service fulfills the enhancement function. The reasons, "volunteering increases my self-esteem," and "volunteering makes me feel better about myself," function as motivation for people to continue their service in order to enhance their personae (see Clary et al., 1998).

Researchers concluded that as long as an act of service functions as the volunteer desires, the volunteer will be motivated to continue serving. Additionally, many volunteers may be motivated by more than one factor depending upon the context of the service. Matching service with its function sustains the willingness of a volunteer to continue with the activity. As soon as the motivational function of the service is no longer being met, the volunteer is likely to discontinue participation. This may explain why volunteers drop out when they do not feel that they are providing the service that first functioned to motivate them to join a club or to serve.

Sustaining the Commitment to Serve

When people engage in service activities over a period of time, they often associate themselves with the activity. For example, those in the medical profession may identify with ongoing service projects related to their expertise as reflected in the following statement: "As an obstetrician and gynecologist, I was a member of Lions Club for more than fifty years and I volunteered especially for eye and umbilical cord bank because I was asked to do it" (6:33). Because others associated the volunteer and his expertise with the service he could provide, he accepted that role when asked to serve.

Role theory is helpful in clarifying how this relationship between interest or expertise and service sustains motivation. As the act of service fulfills its function, the volunteer role is assumed by the individual. Consequently, when people feel their self-esteem rising by volunteering for a specific project, they may be willing to assume the volunteer role again. When the role matches the desired motivation, the volunteer becomes more and more committed to the service perspective. As Finkelstien (2009) described:

> The more others identify one with a particular role, the more the individual internalizes the role and incorporates it into the self-concept ... the role identity guides future behavior as the individual strives to remain consistent with his or her self-concept. Thus, with the development of a volunteer identity, helping becomes not so much what one does, but who one is and is recognized as being. (p. 653)

The assumption of the service role by an individual provides an intrinsic motivator for the volunteer.

The difference between intrinsic and extrinsic motivation is clarified by considering its source. Intrinsic motivation comes from the internal motives of the volunteer. For example, the decision is based upon a personal belief, such as serving is the ethical and moral thing to do. Whereas the extrinsic motivation is characterized as coming from outside of the individual. In this case, the decision is prompted by an external reward, like being able to graduate or winning a prize for service from your company. These relationships suggest that the umbrella of motivational orientation can provide a useful way for understanding the volunteer process.

Recruiting Others to Serve

When people make the decision to volunteer and serve, their motivation often is triggered by the appeals used by the recruiters seeking their help: "The decision to volunteer is a process by which individuals come to see volunteerism in terms of their personal motivations; one way that they can come to view volunteering this way is through exposure to persuasive messages" (Clary et al., 1998, p. 1528). Thus, the matching of persuasive recruitment messages to the motivations or functions sought by the volunteer should enhance their effectiveness in achieving the desired result. In other words, when recruiting individuals to become members of a Lions Club or help with a service project, the messages should focus on what will be most persuasive. For example, if a recruiter knows that her friend has been lamenting the fact that she doesn't know very many people in the community, the recruiter may use an appeal such as: "Please come and help us with this project. It will be a great way to meet some new people and make friends in the community." As long as the volunteer keeps meeting people and making friends, she likely will continue participating in the service projects. Similarly, if potential members are motivated by getting ahead in their careers, the messages to recruit should focus on how service will impress their employers or their clients. If the volunteers are motivated by actions that make them feel better about themselves, the messages should focus on how service contributes to self-worth.

When people identify the reasons why they are motivated to serve, and if they find satisfaction and reward in those reasons, they are likely to continue serving. But, prolonged service will continue only if the recruiters' appeals match what is valued by the recruited individuals and experienced by them over time. Clary and associates referred to this matching process as critical if the appeals are to function as long-term motivators for the volunteer to accept the call to service.

Summary

Previous research on factors that motivate people to volunteer and sustain their commitment to service has shown that people volunteer as a result of a decision-making process whereby they identify an opportunity to serve, perform the service, and evaluate the impact of their actions. Practitioners suggest that in the process of evaluation, volunteers match what motivated them to volunteer with whether or not the service activity functioned as expected. If the act of service and its function match, the likelihood of prolonged commitment to volunteering is greater than if the service fails to satisfy the expectations of the volunteer. With this in mind, what can we learn from the information gathered as part of the survey identifying what sustains a commitment to service over a prolonged period of time?

Robert S. Littlefield

What the Survey Revealed About How Others are Called to Serve

The findings from the survey revealed the commitment of the 791 respondents to prolonged service by asking the question: How long do you think you will continue volunteering or serving the needs of others?[8] The willingness to continue serving as long as they were able reflected the perspective of 621 participants (75 percent). This finding suggests that for those responding, the act of service functioned as a motivator to sustain their commitment. As such, they embraced the role of volunteer.

Table 4.1 provides the breakdown (by language of respondent) of the commitment levels projected by those who responded to the survey. Clearly, the fact that 78.5 percent of the participants declared their intention to serve as long as they were able provides a clear indicator that service functions as an ongoing motivator for them. Since they made a long-term commitment to volunteerism and service, the reasons they offered for use when recruiting volunteers are likely to be reflective of how service functions for them.

---

[8] Of the 716 responses, fifty (7 percent) were unrelated to any of the functions identified. Of these responses, sixteen were missing responses, referenced other answers, or did not understand the question; seventeen provided unrelated personal comments about their lives and perceptions; and seventeen answers were phrases or words provided without context.

Table 4.1

Willingness to Serve Over Time

Length of Service	English	Chinese	Finnish	Japanese	Korean	Portuguese	Spanish	Swedish	Italian	French	German	Total
Up to 1 more year	1	0	2	0	0	0	0	1	2	0	0	6 (.8%)
1-5 yrs more	4	0	15	4	0	4	4	13	6	2	3	55 (6.9%)
6-10 yrs more	10	0	20	8	0	5	3	22	2	12	5	76 (9.6%)
11-15 yrs more	0	0	8	3	0	0	5	7	1	2	1	27 (3.4%)
16-20 yrs more	1	1	1	0	0	0	2	0	0	0	1	6 (.8%)
Long as I am able	66	8	60	29	2	97	107	55	86	70	41	621 (78.5%)
Total responses for each language	82	9	106	44	2	106	121	87	97	86	51	791 (100%)

The respondents then were asked: What reasons would you tell others that could serve to motivate them to begin serving the needs of others? Following this line of thinking, their reasons reflected the functions of service that motivated them most (see Figure 4.1).

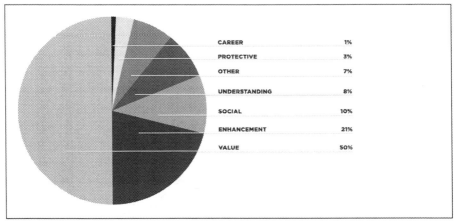

CAREER	1%
PROTECTIVE	3%
OTHER	7%
UNDERSTANDING	8%
SOCIAL	10%
ENHANCEMENT	21%
VALUE	50%

FIGURE 4.1. SELF-IDENTIFIED FUNCTIONS OF SERVICE FOR VOLUNTEERS

Using the VFI, all of the responses from the 716 survey participants were coded and placed into the six functions reflecting the following percentages: value (50 percent), enhancement (21 percent), social (10 percent), understanding (8 percent), protective (3 percent), career (1 percent), and other functions (7 percent). Two independent coders were in total agreement on the identification and placement of these functions into the seven categories. The functions are presented in the order determined by the largest percentage of responses associated with each of them.

Value Function

By far the largest group of reasons used to motivate others to begin serving was related to the values represented in the act of service itself. Out of 716 total responses, 356 (50 percent) indicated that through service, volunteers were able to demonstrate their deeply held values, dispositions, and convictions. The range of responses revealed themes about how serving functioned to reflect these values: Serving helped them do what they believed was right; the duty to serve reflected moral responsibility; service demonstrated concern for broader humanitarian needs; service benefitted everyone, not just the receiver; and service reflected a religious or spiritual orientation to life.

Recognizing the importance of doing the right thing for people in need was often used by respondents as the reason they would use to encourage volunteerism. Examples emerged from the data: "To help is to do the right thing. The price for doing right is incomparable" (4:34); "In every man there is the desire to do good … Address the needs of others, collect the smiles of a child, the tears of a mother, the gratitude of a sick person, all of them are strong motivational elements that correspond with the inmost desire to give" (5:18); and "There is not any better phrase: You cannot go far unless you start by doing something for someone else" (5:41).

Many respondents suggested the moral responsibility or duty to serve those in need was a compelling way for service to demonstrate their values. Selected examples include: "It is the responsibility of the more advantaged to help" (2:54); "The number of people suffering from diverse disabilities on the planet is really important. Lions are privileged and it seems logical, humane, and moral that they support a little part of the happiness to those who have less of it, and sometimes much more less" (3:35); "It is a responsibility of every citizen to take care of people in need. This is called sheer 'god-ness' of one's heart. To rely on the government to take care is not good enough. Our society and economy only work if people do volunteer service and do above the average" (4:9); "I think that if, like many others, we were lucky enough to have a healthy life without major problems, to have received a good education and to have a job and a house, we should look around to where people do not have a job, or a house, or a point of reference. To look at families, affected by natural disasters,

I believe whoever has must look to those who have not" (5:9); "…if we have been privileged and have an opportunity to become better, why not provide help to others because they also deserve love and care" (8:86); "Each person, Lion or not, has to remember that they have to 'walk the walk' not just 'talk the talk'" (11:49); "To share your time with your fellow men—even if it's only a small thing—is the wisest service that is all about kindness rather than being recognized with awards. We must consider service a great privilege rather than a burden" (11:59); and "It is our moral responsibility to help others in our community who are struggling. We make our community stronger by helping others in need to succeed. We need to think about those who do not have the same opportunities as we do. It is an incredible feeling to help a person and to see the joy and gratification on their faces when they succeed" (11:75).

Examples of how respondents used altruistic and humanitarian needs as a way to encourage volunteers to serve were evident. For instance: "We have to love our neighbor and not believe that what is acquired is so forever; never hesitate to question oneself when we face all the sadness that is surrounding us" (3:38); "The best part of life is how you impact others and make their lives better" (11:29); "[Service] is for me the meaning of the word humanity" (3:19); "It is necessary that we work together to collectively make life better for everyone" (10:62); "I believe people were put on this earth to help others and do as much good as they can" (11:5); and "to be at the service of humanity is the most noble work that constitutes a life" (3:11).

The two-way nature of service was evident in some of the responses as participants suggested that giving and receiving service were mutually beneficial. Examples included: "Man lives by emotions. With a single act, you can move two people, the one who receives and your heart" (5:44); "Let's help while we still can! Sometimes we ourselves need some help. When one gives, then there is the possibility to get some needed help oneself" (2:36); "Doing unselfish good work for someone else nurtures and rewards everybody" (2:84); "We all need help in life. Give your help to others and others will help you. When others are down, lift them up and bring JOY to others and JOY will fill your heart" (11:48); and "The world's immense poverty problems are unable to be taken care of other than by establishing significant volunteer service and aid organizations. Yes, and there is certainly joy and content also for one's own life. We can all be great because we can serve one another" (2:28).

The underlying religious and spiritual values of some respondents functioned as the reason or motivation for service. For example: "There are some Chinese traditional cultural attitudes like, 'do more charitable things, god will bless you,' which is the same value as Lions Clubs. With the understanding of Lion culture and background, I believe others would want to volunteer" (1:8); "A metaphor in the Muslim culture says that, 'we are like the organs of the same body; if one of them is sick, all the body is.' So, let's take care of those who are suffering in our society, and let's offer them our help, advice, surrounding … so that they can develop their chances and skills and have a proper life, and so that we can appreciate and enjoy our own luck" (3:6); and "The reason that we should help others is because it is a way of thanking God. To be in peace in this world and feeling happy. Seeing the smiles of the elderly that you helped and the innocent smiles of the kids playing" (10:32).

The volume of responses identifying values as the underlying reason why people serve the needs of others reflected the belief that values function persuasively to motivate people to become volunteers. The responses revealed themes about doing what was right and moral, showing concern for broader humanitarian needs, benefitting both the receiver and giver of service, and supporting a religious or spiritual orientation to life. Following the use of values as a motivator, the next most frequent response identified the enhancement function of service.

Enhancement Function

In contrast to the value function where people demonstrated their commitment to serving the needs of others as their motivation, the enhancement function focuses on those elements of service that promote the individual's growth and development. Some 154 responses out of 716 total (21 percent) indicated that service produced positive feelings that enhanced their own personal views of themselves. Several themes were identified from their responses, including: increased self-esteem, increased satisfaction, and gaining a sense of purpose.

The increased self-esteem resulting from service was revealed numerous times by respondents with the simple sentence: It feels good to serve. Other examples included the following: "The feeling of pleasure that comes when you realize that you have been useful to someone less fortunate" (5:57); "From making others happy, I also become happy" (6:35); "You can increase your self-esteem when you volunteer, meet new people, and see the real meaning of family—not from blood but from affection" (8:29); "It is a good feeling to help others" (9:18); and "It is an opportunity for me to accumulate some merits, when you could see their lives improved significantly with your help" (1:9).

Another aspect of enhancement was the positive feeling associated with satisfaction. Multiple respondents used the gaining of personal satisfaction as the result of service. For example: "Satisfaction comes from helping" (8:13). Other instances included: "Voluntary work comes from everyone's innermost being. When you know, and feel that you can be of help to someone somewhere and see the result of work done for the good of the neighbor, it gives new strength for the new task" (2:30); "Helping others causes us personal satisfaction and makes us feel happier" (8:82); "gratefulness and satisfaction" (10:2); "There is nothing more satisfying than being able to serve and assist someone less fortunate than yourself" (11:42); and "Internal motivation is particularly rewarding. The feeling from doing the right things is empowering" (2:27).

Finally, gaining a sense of purpose was identified as a theme of enhancement by the respondents. Examples of how service was tied to purpose were evident: "One gets a good feeling from helping and the feeling that my life has meaning" (2:15); "It brings joy and meaning to oneself at the same time as it helps a neighbor" (2:65); "It makes you more complete as a person, especially for a non-religious person like me it is worthwhile contemplating one's own position in the world and in relationship to others" (3:16); "Feeling of accomplishment for a better world" (8:43); "It makes you feel very, very content after helping the needy" (10:74).

"It makes you feel alive" (10:70); "It enriches one's life! Martin Buber [scholar and philosopher] wrote: 'Man wird am du zu ich'" [trans. "It is on you and I."] (11:25); and "Serving the needs of others gives me purpose, one of the reasons I exist. It is the way to give back" (11:40).

These statements functioning as enhancement for an individual's growth and development reflected the second largest body of responses to the question of what reasons would motivate potential volunteers to begin serving the needs of others. Enhancing self-esteem, increasing satisfaction, and gaining a sense of purpose provided overarching themes representing the participants' responses. After personal enhancement, the next most frequent function involved being included in social groups with one's friends or engaged in an activity viewed favorably by others.

Social Function

Of the 716 total responses, seventy-three (10 percent) suggested that service functioned to help people fit socially with important reference groups. Specifically, being with both new and established friends, family, Lions Clubs, and other social connections were identified as reasons why a person should participate in service projects.

For some, service functioned as a way to be together with both new and established friends. For example: "One gets many good new friends! Helping is spiritually rewarding" (2:43); "so something useful with friends" (3:30); "[service] is something to do together, have good friends" (4:2); "It is interesting and you get to know so many new people outside of your group" (9:6); "[I serve] because of the community in our group—friends—and to be able to meet new people and at the same time help make the world a better place" (9:26); "the community you experience and the friends you meet in the organization" (9:40, 9:44); and "Make new unexpected friends" (11:55).

Being together with family is another way service fulfills a social function. Examples of these references include: "…Lions is great for family. When my daughters were younger, they would come and help with our projects. So, one would not need a babysitter in order to come to our projects or meetings" (11:11); and "Since I was little, I would take part in the programs and I fell in love with the club" (10:38).

Many responses identified that becoming a member of Lions Club enabled them to participate in service projects, fulfilling the social function for them. Other comments included: "It makes it easier to be in a group of people volunteering. That's why it is important for me to be a member of Lions. Together we do more than any of us could achieve on our own" (9:12); "People cannot live alone. I have a relationship with many people who are my family, friends, and people from the community. That is why I participate in Lions Club—whatever I can do and I think that is what everyone should do" (6:7); "The community in Lions Club is enough of a motivation" (9:33); and "Many of the people that I work with are isolated and the Lions Club would provide a supportive community and allow them to get involved in helping others" (11:61).

Gaining broader social or community connections also was used as a reason for becoming involved with service. Examples included the general reason "for social association" (2:37), but also suggest that service provides "the necessary community and solidarity to face any type of difficulty; the richness to enrich our own human experience with positive relationships with other people ... The feeling to be part of a group that invests with passion for the good of the community (economic, emotional, for special events)" (5:38)

The inclusion of a reasons supporting the social function of service underlines the benefits gained by volunteering with friends, family, Lions Clubs, and with other like-minded members of the community.

Understanding Function

There were fifty-six responses out of 716 (8 percent) suggesting that by becoming a volunteer, service functions as a way to increase knowledge and understanding. The responses were grouped into two categories: Volunteering functions as a way to demonstrate knowledge, skills, and abilities that might otherwise go unpracticed; and through service, volunteers gain understanding of the changing world.

Many of the responses supported the theme that volunteering functions as a way to exercise ability or knowledge that might otherwise go unpracticed. Examples reflected the positive effect of understanding: "Sharing your collaboration and success helps us to grow together" (1:7); "[Serving] enriches yourself ... by getting interested in another country or continent. Being open to different cultures. Being understood by the others so that our actions are useful and last in time. Evolving in our ethical reflection is essential here and abroad" (3:52); "Joining an NGO like Lions Club or Rotary [enables you] to learn and improve the service of those in need, have a better vision for your community, and ensures hard work" (8:44); "[Service] is an experience that changes one's life and teaches us to give to those less fortunate ... by making a difference in their lives" (10:10); "It's always our goal to find out where we fit in life and to make us grow and there is no better place than to be helping people in need" (10:26); and "It's about having an objective in life. Have plans, not only to yourself but also to those around you. I believe that people that have plans, live better" (8:50).

The respondents also indicated their perception that service would function to provide an understanding of a changing world for potential volunteers. Examples of the learning gained from this broader knowledge included: "Volunteering opens our eyes on other worlds beyond the microcosm in which we live. It permits us to be useful to the ones who are in need. The volunteer actions, usually made with a team are very rewarding" (3:80); "Today's society is very complex and it is going through a very difficult time ... The most important objective is to make people understand that my wealth (prosperity), depends and is influenced from happiness and riches of other people. A service organization must be able to communicate this principle. If one can do so, it can be much easier to join in" (5:7); "We are all citizens of a single community. Each individual development is a development for all humanity. A volunteering opportunity will return as being successful, for the whole society and then for ourselves" (5:60); "Enrich yourself through exchange by getting interested in another country or continent. Being opened to different cultures. Being understood by the others so that our actions are useful and last in time ... Evolving in our ethical reflection is essential here and abroad" (3:52); and "Being engaged in the service of others gives a meaning to life" (3:63).

For the 8 percent of the respondents who used understanding as the function for motivating others to service, their reasons suggested that volunteering would give recruits the chance to demonstrate their capabilities and gain a broader understanding of the world.

Protective Function

There were twenty responses out of 716 total (3 percent) who suggested that service functioned as a defense to reduce guilt about being more fortunate than others. The comments used to recruit volunteers centered on the theme of helping to keep personal problems in perspective. All of the examples reflected this sentiment: "There are way more people on the planet with bigger problems that yours. That's why we should donate our time to help our community and with the challenges that life gives to you" (8:9); "We all have issues, but when we face problems way bigger than ours, we feel blessed by God, so it's impossible not to share a bit of what we have, even if a little bit of money, a smile, a little bit of time or a simple gentle word" (8:76); "We should be grateful for what we have. There are a lot of people and communities that have so little. Helping many people is the blessing that you are getting, knowing that God is watching you has no price" (10:86); "When you give your time to people that are for some reason disadvantaged, one feels good themselves and can put things in their own lives into perspective with the right measurements ... Lions activity brings a good counterbalance to daily work" (2:6); and "By rendering service we do good to ourselves, we become aware of the difficulties the other can encounter. We put into perspective the difficulties we go through" (3:17).

Career Function

Only seven responses out of 716 total (1 percent) reflected utilitarian attitudes about using service as a means for self-advancement or career-related benefits from participating in volunteer work. Some of the benefits of service included "international contacts" (2:55) and "the feeling of social cohesion and networking" (2:85). Being a member of the local group also afforded one of the respondents the opportunity to be involved with local investors, "very often a deep relationship" (3:68).

Conclusion

Clary and associates (1998) found that, "people can be recruited into volunteer work by appealing to their own psychological functions, ... and that they will plan to continue to serve as volunteers to the extent that their psychological functions are being served by their service" (p. 1518). Because over 78 percent of the participants indicated they planned to continue serving as long as they were able, I concluded that this commitment to prolonged service must be based upon reasons that continue to motivate them. Thus, when asked "what reasons would you tell others to motivate them to begin serving the needs of others," their responses should provide the reasons that motivated them to serve. By using the VFI, the responses from the 716 survey participants were coded and then prioritized based upon the functions perceived to be most important. Service to demonstrate values received the highest support (50 percent), followed by personal enhancement (21 percent), social relationships (10 percent), increased understanding (8 percent), protection in the form of keeping problems in perspective (3 percent), and career enhancement (1 percent).

In chapter 4, identifying the reasons that motivate others to accept the call to serve has reflected the priorities of volunteers who themselves have made a lifetime commitment. But making the decision to volunteer and knowing in your heart that you will always be committed to serving the needs of others are two different experiences. In the next chapter, one hundred personal stories are presented to show how the epiphany of a true commitment to service was experienced by Lions who opened their hearts to the needs of others.

Lions Club member planting tree in Chian Mai Thailand 1975-1985

Lions Club of Nkana presents Diabetes Awareness Week 1982

Chapter 5

Stories from the Servant's Heart

"As an individual, I started supporting a child living in the orphanage in 1972 and continued until he graduated from a university. When he was going to marry, he asked me to officiate his wedding. In Korea, the wedding officiant is usually chosen from among the most respected and venerable men, mostly over 60. However, my age at that time was just 36. I was touched and felt rewarded for my love and efforts. What I realized through my volunteer work was that we do serve people in need and when the need is filled, we can see their growth and happiness and ours as well." (Lion Joong-ho Son)

The story of Lionism is a not a single narrative. Rather, Lionism is a collection of stories as diverse as the millions of members who have joined the association over its one-hundred-year history. This chapter includes the stories of one hundred Lions—symbolically presenting one story for every year of Lions Clubs International's history—revealing the way that an act of service touches the heart and can change a person's life. These one hundred stories demonstrate how service is a powerful, compelling motivation for accepting the principles of Lionism as a cultural orientation for life.

The question used to gather the stories was, "please share a story that has meaning to you about when you felt in your heart that your service made a difference in the life of someone in need." The one hundred stories included in this chapter were selected from a pool of 758 stories provided through interviews, an online survey, and invitations extended to individuals at district, multiple district, and international levels. In addition to the initial face-to-face interviews, a variety of social media were used by LCI to encourage participation. The stories taken from the online survey were entered anonymously in order to safeguard the identity of the participants who provided them. The stories without named authors are identified by referencing the language and participant number, as was described in chapter 1. The stories gathered through interviews or in response to online invitations are identified with the names of the Lions who gave their permission for attribution.

Several factors influenced the selection of the stories for inclusion. Effort was made to include stories reflecting LCI's international composition. The stories of Lions who are known for their contributions to LCI were prioritized for inclusion. All stories needed to meet a more important criterion; that is, the stories had to reveal a compelling and readily apparent moment of epiphany for the storyteller. Through a process of constant comparison, the selected stories were those that made the author want to go back and read them again and again.

The epiphanies were not uniform. The storytellers may have experienced their moment when they personally observed something giving meaning to their service. They may have come to realize in a new way that individually, they made a difference in someone's life. They may have done something that they never had undertaken before and felt empowered by their efforts. For some, the intangible gift of empathy—experiencing an emotion found in the response of the recipient—provided a life-changing moment; while for others, being inspired by observing the gift of service altered their outlook on themselves and their future place in the world. Setting aside some of the stories was difficult; each provided a glimpse into the heart of the storyteller. Thus, the stories included in this chapter were carefully chosen, and represent unique perspectives on the gift of service from the heart.

For the remainder of this chapter, the one hundred stories are loosely grouped by type and provided without additional commentary. The stories speak for themselves and reveal elements of the culture of Lionism: Being able to communicate with or without words; having an inherent intent to be helpful; being willing to help others without knowing the identity or background of those in need; and having a worldview that reflects the power of personal and organizational agency to change or improve the lives of those in need. The chapter concludes with an affirmation of this cultural orientation to service.

The One Hundred Stories

When I Experienced the Service

"He could go to school like the other children."

I went on my first eye glass mission to Latvia in 2004 and that's when I came to realize the true impact Lions have in our world. At that time, children needed to know how to read before they could start school and we had a mother come to the clinic with her seven-year-old son who was not in school because he could not read. Our eye exam showed that he desperately needed glasses and thankfully, we were able to fill his prescription. After he was fitted for the glasses, he had a wonderful smile on his face and his mother began to cry because now, he could see and he could learn how to read. He could go to school like the other children. That experience is one that stays with me daily and one that continues to reinforce why I'm a Lion. I returned to Latvia on two more eye glass missions in 2006 and 2008. (Lion Esther LaMothe)

"They wait all year long to 'climb new mountains.'"

Because I come from a family of Lions, with both of my parents, my husband, and my daughter being Lions prior to my induction, I believe that I experienced some *aha!* moments before I became a member. One of my first recollections was visiting Beacon Lodge, our special needs camp for children and adults. This is a beautiful facility in the mountains of central Pennsylvania where children and adults spend one or two weeks as 'normal' individuals. Every year, on the third Sunday of July, the camp sponsors Lions Appreciation Day when we can tour the wonderful facilities, walk the braille trail, try our luck at miniature golf, rock climbing, or the zip line, eat a barbequed chicken dinner, and enjoy a fabulous show delivered by the campers. Regardless of the number of times that I have visited, I am always amazed as they share their outstanding talents with the Lions, Lioness, Leos, and guests. While it is generally the hottest day of summer, these campers sing as if they were on Broadway. In fact, I believe that some of them have the talent to be on *American Idol* or *America's Got Talent*. Yet, when they thank the Lions from the bottom of their heart for this wonderful experience, it is difficult to hold back the tears. This is their vacation. They wait all year long to *climb new mountains*, to rekindle friendships, to make new ones, and to share their talents with those who help to support the camp. (Lion Cindy Gregg)

"Tears of joy from sight regained"

I was invited to join the Lions club in 1975 by my dentist when I was twenty-seven years old. My dentist was a member of the board of education and I had just become principal of the local school in Daleville, Alabama. To be honest, I made the decision to join for purely selfish reasons. It was the premier club in the community; well-respected and recognized. I thought it would be good for my career. The club had an excellent indoctrination program; and I got involved in district and club activities; going to district meetings and participating in local community service projects. It wasn't until three years later when I truly learned what it meant to be a Lion. There was a lady in the community who needed to have surgery; and at that time, the eye surgery was only offered at an eye hospital in Birmingham, sponsored by the Lions of Alabama's statewide sight foundation. Clubs had to provide transportation for patients who would stay for a week, and then were returned to their home. I could not go when our club took her; but I was able to bring her home. The hospital had taken a video of her when the doctors took the patches off her eyes. The video was a black and white, grainy video. But, I got to see the patch removed by the ophthalmologist and to see her reaction of being able to see. Tears streamed down her face. I have since seen similar experiences in China; but this was in 1978 and the surgery was not common. It was extraordinary at that time. That experience, of being able to see that video, and listening to her as she talked the entire way home—three hours— about what Lions had done for her and how it would change her life and family; that really did have an impact on me. It was when being a Lion really hit home. I'll never forget it. That was my recognition that we do tremendous things for people. (Lion J. Frank Moore)

"All we did was give a meal."

When I was first invited to join the Lions Club, I thought "here is another group that just wants all of my time." But I said I'd go to the meeting and I was impressed. One night, a group of men were sitting around a table planning to deliver meals for Thanksgiving. We were going in pairs, and I volunteered. The other Lion carried the twenty-pound turkey and I carried a laundry basket with all the trimmings. We rang the doorbell and introduced ourselves as members of the local Lions Club. We told the mother who opened the door that the food was for her family. She stood there with tears in her eyes and said, "Thank you. No one has ever done anything for my family." I was touched in my heart. I looked around and saw how they lived and said, "there but for the grace of God." I left feeling so good about what we'd done; and all we'd done was to give a meal to a needy family. That was the day when I became a Lion. (Lion Douglas Alexander)

"We baked them cookies at Christmas."

What really touches my heart in Lions is the people and what we do with those in palliative care in Regina. Each year, we make Christmas cookies and bring them to the people. There's not a dry eye in the house. We also supply them with picture calendars so they can see the beautiful scenes from the area. It makes me so happy to help people in this way. (Lion Maureen Meston Pockett)

"Glasses of faith"

The story that really caught my heart happened to one of my fellow Lions when he was doing an eye screening test. He did an eye screening test for the elderly, and when it came time to give the glasses to the elderly, there was one man who hugged him particularly tight and with tears in his eyes. He said, "Thank you sir, thank you very much. My glasses were broken around one year ago, and I couldn't afford to buy a new one. Now, I can see clearly again. Now, I can read the bible again. I haven't read it since my glasses were broken. I know that God has listened to my prayer. Thank you, sir." This is one of the reasons why I become a Lion. I am looking forward to serving more people, to collect more stories, to collaborate with other clubs, and even other districts, and try to make this world a little bit friendlier to those who are less fortunate. At last, allow me to quote from Ralph Waldo Emerson, "To know even one life has breathed easier because you have lived. This is to have succeeded." (Lion Anthony Salim)

"A school for Kemba"

A Lions Club, *Acqui Terme*, and a school for the village of Kemba located just below the equatorial forest in the Democratic Republic of Congo where the boys were studying in a hut, sitting on the ground with a roof that was not sheltered from rain. Three events were organized by the Club: an immediate response that helped in gathering the 35,000 dollars that, with an equal amount of an LCIF grant, allowed for the construction of a school with twelve classrooms, two headmasters, a teacher's lounge and a library, at the service of more than 500 children. I've been twice in the village of Kemba, reached Kinshasa after an hour-and-a-half flight landing on a road, then three hours in a small boat on the river Likenie, and finally with a jeep ride fifty miles inside the Savannah. The first time in February 2012 was to lay the first stone. I was greeted by a jubilant village with singing and dancing because the Lions were bringing joy and social progress. The second time in November 2013, I went together with the District Governor of District 409 to inaugurate the facility. I was welcomed not only as a Lion but also as a friend, with the hug—long and loud—of the village chief. In the following months, I was informed that many mothers had named their sons Robert, the Lion who had been twice to the village. Why?

Only one answer, to give a future of hope for their children. Yes, because Lions bring hope for a better life. (Lion Roberto Fresia)

"Suddenly language was no longer a barrier."

During my twenty-nine years as a Lion, I have traveled to ninety-three countries. Upon each visit, I was blessed with the rare opportunity to witness thousands of the millions of miracles undertaken by the members of our great association each year. I find it overwhelmingly difficult to identify the story that stood out most, as each touched my soul in a special way. However, I do recall a particular incident that remained locked in my memory and that always arises when I think of what inspired me most. Twenty years ago, while on a trip to Pakistan as International Director with my wife Alia, we visited several projects including an extension of a small school for girls. We drove into the northern part of the country for hours, after which we had to cross by foot a certain distance to reach the site of the event. Upon our arrival, about forty young girls dressed in their uniforms welcomed us with a greeting song. Although we could not understand the language, and therefore what the song was about, we were deeply moved by the joy expressed by these girls towards the extension of their school. Suddenly language was no longer a barrier. This project was special: the girls were divided into three classes. However, the structure was made of two modest rooms. The girls would then have to rotate with two groups occupying two rooms while the third group waited outside enduring winter's bitter cold and summer's burning heat. I recall with fondness until today the building of the foundation of the third room, and witnessing the happiness of the girls. That is the power of "*We Serve!*" and that is the interpretation of "*Where there is a need there is a Lion.*" (Lion Salim Moussan)

"His very own toothbrush"

One of my club's Christmas traditions was to bring gift bags to all the elementary-school-aged children the last day before the Christmas break. Our community is economically depressed and not all the kids had hats and mittens to wear during the freezing winter. We knew on most wintery days the school would allow the kids to play outside for breaks. In our gift bags, we had hats and mittens for each child along with some small games and tokens. One of the tokens this particular year included toothbrushes. Lion Bill and I volunteered to bring the bags to school in our Santa hats. We cheerfully passed out the gift bags. The children had to wait to open until all had a bag. The bags were opened and many were trying on their hats and mittens, squealing with delight. One child near the front was bouncing up and down and started squealing loudly, more so than the other kids. He stood up and started stamping his feet and crying, all the other children started looking at him to see what he had received. The teacher came over to him, kneeled down and said, "Johnny, what's the matter." Johnny, crying, looked at the teacher holding out his toothbrush and said, "Teacher, I got my own toothbrush. I don't have to share with my sister anymore." Lion Bill and I looked at each other and saw we both had tears in our eyes. (Lion Bruce Beck)

"A line of local villagers as if they were waiting for a carnival"

Imagine a line of local villagers. The adults in their threadbare clothes and the children with dirt smudged faces and bare feet. All of them waiting anxiously for their turn. Sounds like they should be waiting for a carnival ride or some other exciting event. Well for them, this is an exciting event. It is the day that they get their annual dose of antibiotics to help prevent trachoma. You see, every one of these people have been impacted by trachoma in some way. It is the number one cause of blindness in their region. So, they gladly line up for their chance to see the local healthcare volunteer. The children are measured with a stick to determine their height and then given the appropriate dose based on the measurement. The adults receive a standard dose. The healthcare volunteer then records the administration and moves on to the next family. This scene can be seen all over the Amhara region of Ethiopia. Over the course of one week there will be twenty-one million doses of antibiotics administered. This is just one of the many amazing projects Lions are doing all over the world. I only wish that every

Lion could experience this first hand. To see the relief on the faces of those villagers when they know that they will be spared the pain and suffering and potential blindness of trachoma. Seeing projects like this has changed our lives forever. (Lion Joe & Lion Joni Preston)

"A small window of joy"

My most profound life-changing experience as a Lion occurred just recently. Our Lions club chose to partner with the Friends of Ft. Lincoln in providing a safe, family-friendly Halloween party. The day was beautiful and as my husband and I arrived there was already a long line of people waiting to get in. We quickly took our stations, mine was the board where children reached into the circle to get a prize. Because these children were quite young, we had decided that all of the prizes would be candy with some grand prizes awarded to ride the Lions train. About an hour into the event, a family of four children with mom and dad approached my game. The two older children quickly took their turns of reaching into the hole to receive their prizes and then they assisted their younger sibling. I noticed that the little girl that I assumed was around four years old, had a difficult time seeing the objects in front of her and that she tilted her head to the side. Since I am a trained vision screener, I engaged in a conversation with the parents asking them where their children attended school and offering the Lions free vision screening program to them. It was then that her mother shared that her daughter had an inoperable brain tumor. In that moment, my life was changed forever. Not only did we achieve our goal in providing a safe and family friendly event. We provided this family with a small window of joy during their time of crisis. We provided happiness in a time of hopelessness. For that great honor, I am most grateful. (Lion Patricia "Pat" Vannett)

"Playgrounds, parks, and wheelchair ramps"

The club I am a part of mainly works with public parks and playground projects. We also install wheelchair ramps in areas that aren't accessible to the handicapped all around our community. While the work can be grueling at times, when I drive past a playground that I helped build, I am able to see a tangible difference that I made. Watching the children stay active and build friendships and memories is the most rewarding part of it. (11:39)

"A new sense of freedom"

A seven-year-old blind girl refused to consider a service dog, even though it would be a great help to her. She was very afraid of dogs due to a negative experience she had when she was very young. We had invited her to a few events where we had service dogs available along with their foster owner. During the event, she started to move closer and closer to the young black service lab until she was willing to touch the dog. We linked her up with the dog's foster parent and she is slowly but surely changing her attitude towards the service dog. Her grandmother is now looking into the program for her granddaughter. When she is connected to a service dog her independence and environment will be much more open to her and she will gain a new sense of freedom. (11:29)

"A little boy's independence"

I can tell you about one young boy who got a seeing eye dog when he was twelve years old. He could go outside by himself for the first time and he was so overjoyed and full of tears that it brought tears to my eyes. Moments like that keep me in Lions. I have been a Lion for twenty-seven years and like I always say, if you've been a Lion for more than twenty years, you're a Lion for life. I can guarantee I will be a Lion for the rest of my life. (Lion Bill Hackett)

"Covered in barbeque sauce"

Taking people in wheelchairs for a barbeque was an amazing experience. I helped push them for a fair distance all the way to the venue. With lots of effort and fun we all did it together. In addition to getting them to the barbeque, I assisted with helping some of them eat and drink. To hold a cup for someone who can't do it himself is an experience one has to go through himself to fully understand. The happiness on their faces showed they felt more accepted in life than they usually do. We were all happily covered in delicious barbeque sauce. This was an experience that will be with me for life. (11:68)

"The beauty in life"

I'm a Past President of the Florida Lions Foundation for the Blind. We provide surgeries to people in need to save their sight. The cases that get me the most emotional are when we can assist children who have problems with their eyes and we are able to restore their sight. I cannot imagine what it would be like to miss out on all the visual beauty of the world and I am glad these children will not have to experience that. (11:42)

"We filled the 'flat'"

Every year, my Lions Club (Dolbeau-Mistassini, Quebec, Canada), organizes an event that consists of distributing grocery baskets to the less well-off before Christmas. When I arrived at the family where I had to give the basket, I realized how poor they were. Almost no furniture. When I went back to the Club, I discussed how all of us Lions could search in our attics to find furniture and things that we didn't use any more. We filled the 'flat' of the family … and I saw the tears of joys of the parents and the children. It was from that moment I decided to try to change the conditions of living for people just with the little things I could provide. (3:25)

"You could see the children burst with happiness"

I have many stories to tell. Among them, I would like to mention my participation in a small service for abandoned and misfit children admitted to an orphanage in the city where I live. We brought during the Christmas

Holidays, small and perhaps trivial gifts. After the delivery of those gifts, you could see the children burst with happiness, indeed they were touched. For me it was a wonderful evening. (5:63)

"I saw in their eyes so much joy."

There are so many stories! I remember some holidays (Christmas and Epiphany) where I spent time with children from a foster home. These children had handicaps or were without parents. We asked each child what he or she wanted as gifts. We brought to them many gifts. Together we partied, bringing them pizzas, hotdogs, chocolate cakes, and various drinks. I saw in their eyes so much joy. Pieces of togetherness. I was happy because I was able to make them smile. (5:77)

"His eyes wept with emotion."

Many years ago, in 1970, there was a disastrous flooding in my city, Genoa. Many died or were injured. Houses and shops were destroyed. Lions were asked to help the citizens. I offered myself to help those that in just a moment had lost everything. We were shoveling mud, and I saw with my own eyes, a picture and different image from what you see on television. In fact, persons were desperate, but I particularly remember an elderly person who upon seeing me, wept with emotion because of what we young people were doing to help; and even if it did nothing more, we were willing to help save what little was left. (5:82)

"I was touched by children's shining eyes."

I knew I was a Lion when I donated to an elementary school in Cambodia twenty years ago. That was my first voluntary activity overseas. At the opening ceremony, not only children but also most of the people from the local area came. After visiting Cambodia four times, and in my fifth visit in Vietnam this year for a child education facility endowment, I was touched by children's shining eyes and pride in reestablishing their own country. I believe children's education is the most important thing to stand up for after disastrous domestic conflicts. (6:3)

"Our efforts give them self-esteem."

I became a Lion when I saw that even small actions, such as organizing and creating a community garden for a school can inspire children to work as a team. In return, we receive smiles and happiness. Our efforts give them self-esteem and a good experience because they can feel they did something with their own hands. (8:5)

"Teacher! I see, I see!"

I participated in the first Lion's eye operation (1969) and I was impressed by giving small children glasses. Seeing them jump for joy, saying: "Teacher! I see, I see!" From that moment on, I have been a Lion without any interruptions. (10:76)

Realizing One Person Can Make a Difference

"He told me we saved that boy's life."

When people ask "Why did you join Lions?" I always respond truthfully. To play golf. My club met at noon and had a standing tee time following the meeting at 1:30. While I participated in nearly every service project my primary purpose for attending meetings was to play golf afterward. That changed the year I became club president. We conducted a vision screening and found a boy who was desperately in need of vision therapy. He was in the lowest reading group in his class and received grades of C and below. He was recommended for Special Education. I spoke with his mother about the importance of enrolling him in a vision therapy program. She was low income and tearfully responded that she could not afford the ten sessions at one hundred US dollars per session. I spoke with the club board of directors who agreed we should help but we would require a commitment from the mother. I asked her if she could contribute ten US dollars per session. She said she would find it. One evening a few months later I received a call from the doctor who conducted the vision therapy. He told me we saved that boy's life. He advanced to the highest reading group and improved his grades to A's and B's. A few days later we received a letter from the mother with his picture at graduation and a note from him thanking us for making that possible. After reading the letters to the club there was not a dry eye in the room. That day I truly learned what it met to be a Lion. Golf was not quite as important that afternoon. (Lion Jack Epperson)

"The best part is we can hear our Mom's voice ..."

I joined the Lions Club in October 1973. After a couple of years, I was appointed to the Hearing Committee. In 1976, the club received a request for hearing aid assistance for twin five-year-old boys. I got to recommend approval of their applications and process them on to the audiologist for their exams and the fitting of mounds for their ears. I felt really good about my part in helping these two boys to be able to hear, as they were about to start kindergarten. Yet, I still hadn't become a Lion. Two months later, the club received a letter from the boys written with the help of their Mom. She expressed their heartfelt thanks for their aids. The boys described their daily trek to school. They talked about the first time they heard the robin singing in the trees, the scampering sound of the squirrels climbing through the branches. Did you know that candy wrappers make a lot of noise? "The best part is that we can hear our Mom's voice and the many voices we never heard for five years." Realizing the impact my Lions Club and I had on the lives of these boys directly gave me chills then and still does. I know I helped someone to have a much better life and future. (Lion Melvyn K. Bray)

"The red feather fundraiser that saved the man's sight"

When I joined Lions twenty-five year ago, I thought I was a real Lion. But, I became a Lion in my heart about a year later, when I realized the impact of how Lions can really change lives. I was for the first time selling the *Red Feather,* a national fundraiser. I was not happy about walking door to door selling a useless thing. But then I got the motivation needed. I knocked on one door and a gentleman opened. I told him I was a Lion and selling ... and he interrupted me, and said: "I know Lions, I thank Lions for what I am today." He told me his story. When he was young, studying at the University, he contracted an eye disease and almost went blind. His sight could be saved with an operation, but the hospital did not have the equipment. He needed to go abroad to a bigger eye clinic, but he could not afford it, and his sight got worse. Suddenly, he got a call from the hospital. The Lions in Iceland had—with the first Red Feather fundraiser in 1972—bought the equipment for the new eye clinic, and he was to be the first patient. He said: "Lions saved my sight, I finished my studies and have since then worked as a scientist for a better world. I thank Lions for my sight and my career." How proud I was of the Lions' impact; how we can change lives and how that can change the world. (Lion Gudrun Yngvadottir)

"I had become a Lion's Lion."

All my life I was a joiner and participated in leadership roles. By the age of thirty I had many. So, when asked to join the Lions Club my answer was: "When you start one in Arkdale, I'll join." Then it happened. I had many business dealings with Clarence Sturm (forty-third International President). He made sure we had a club. As I was going to our first meeting, I told my wife, "I'll join but I won't take an office." I was voted in as Vice President. After my presidency, I was appointed Zone Chair, then onto District Governor and Council Chair. Next was to be voted onto the Board of Directors of our Wisconsin Lions Foundation, and that led to being president of the board. I had really become a Lion's Lion. I was elected as an international director in 1987. The international board zeros in on one great theme, blindness. We made our Wisconsin Lions Camp a year-round facility, started the Vitamin A project, and began a partnership with the Lions of Mexico that is now called Wisconsin Missions. As a reluctant starter in Lionism, it sure grows on you. (Lion Helmer Lecy)

"She was calling out to everyone that she could finally see."

I became acquainted with Lions in 1975 when my husband joined. For the next twelve years, I helped with fundraisers and programs before I was able to become a Lion on June 1, 1987. I wanted to join as soon as possible because I saw that Lions were grassroots people who performed service in a hands-on way. The sight service programs were wonderful. I was able to help give the incredible gift of sight through the sponsorship of eye exams, glasses, and surgical procedures for both children and adults. I knew that I was committed to serving the needs of others when a little girl our club provided glasses to ran through the hall of the school the day she got her glasses calling out to everyone that she could see. When I heard this from her mom I knew I was a Lion and we had contributed something immeasurable to this child and I want to continue to be part of this great work for the rest of my life. (Lion Barbara Jean Heath)

"The profound significance of service"

In 1979 I was transferred from Johnson City, Tennessee, to Spartanburg, South Carolina, to fill the position of Dean of Students of a small business school. Shortly after I arrived, I decided I wanted to purchase a home and my employer suggested that I contact a particular realtor which I did. During one of the showings, the realtor invited me to attend his Lions club. I, of course, at the time didn't know what a Lions Club was nor what they did. I didn't even know if it was a social or service organization. I did attend and found it to be a friendly group of individuals that made me feel welcome. Over the next several weeks I was again invited by the same Lion to visit the club, and each time I felt more welcomed by the members. At some point in time I was invited to be a member. I attended meetings regularly and participated in fundraising activities, but it was not until I attended the South Carolina School for the Deaf and Blind's

Christmas party that I truly understood the significance of service that Lions do. I found out later that my home club had been buying Christmas gifts for those children for over seventy-five years. The children were so appreciative, and for some, this was the only gift they would receive for Christmas. The next year we took our six-year-old daughter. Today our daughter is forty-one years old and still remembers the time she attended the Christmas party at the School for the Deaf and Blind. It was then that I realized why I became a Lion and how it changed my life. (Lion Eugene Spiess)

"Her eyes remained motionless."

I have had the privilege of working with the passionate Lions and health professionals for Lions SightFirst China Action (SFCA) program, and travelled to many impoverished regions in China. It was an unforgettable journey when I witnessed countless touching stories and realized the value of humanitarian service in Lionism. Tibet was one of the project sites and has high prevalence of cataracts due to high altitude and prolonged UV radiation exposure. In the early 2000s, many Tibetans were still living in the dark with limited access to healthcare. There we met a family; the mother, her daughter and younger son, all were born blind. The father suffered this tragedy and left without return. We prioritized treatment for the son which was a total success. However, the daughter given her older age (ten-year old) had less chance of recovery. Facing the disappointed child, we did not give up hope. After surgery we gathered, the doctor uncovered her eye mask. Her eyes remained motionless. There was the long silence. Not until the daughter smelled the boiled eggs and grabbed one did we cry tears of happiness. She saw for the first time. I always remember the thrill of joy when the daughter and many other patients experienced restored vision. It changed their lives and allowed their families to return to daily activities and hence escape from poverty. In SFCA phase I—II (1997–2007), Lions supported over 5.2 million cataract operations in China. The project achievements were accepted and recognized by the Chinese government. It aroused public awareness and sped up the development of eye care service in China. Let's start with small steps. We all can make a big difference to the world. (Lion Wing Kun Tam)

"Nothing is impossible."

As we lose ourselves in the service of others, we discover our own lives, our own happiness. With one year of my Presidency in Lions Club of Hyderabad Cosmo-316 F, with great support of my District Governor V T Rajkumar, Region Chair Kamal Rathi and Zone Chair K. Gopal and along with the efforts of many hands anxiously engaged for a good cause, we broke the records of smiles created through service. As a club, we not only lit the lamp in a few people's lives, but also brightened our own path. Collecting 10k units of blood for thalasemic patients, conducting 400 activities on the same day for children dedicated to our founder Melvin Jones, doing 11,000 plus Lionistic activities and 35 percent membership growth is my most satisfying story as a Lion who always believed in building the brand of Lionism. Personally, with twenty-five years into Lionism, I always enjoyed serving as well as the LCI leadership trainings which changed the course of my life. Through Lionism I learned that nothing is impossible, that a candle has the power to both defy and define light, that each one of us has the extraordinary power to make the world a better place, that love in action is service and that we only grow rich by giving. Long Live Lionism! (Lion S K Ram Mohan)

"A fire for service cannot burn out."

For many years, I owned a cottage in Wisconsin and was a charter member of the Lake Wisconsin Lions Club that was formed by both local citizens and weekend visitors like myself. After selling my cottage, I slowly drifted away from Lionism and finally ended my membership. Not too many years later after coming very close to losing my vision due to retina detachments in both eyes, I developed a feeling that something was missing from my life. Suddenly, and without warning, the *We Serve!* fire that resides in the hearts of all Lions burst into flames in mine and I joined the Elgin Lions Club in Illinois. Since that day, I have made it a point to be very active in my club and have concentrated on participating in as many club programs and activities as possible. That fire never went out and now it continues to burn brightly. (Lion William Klawitter)

"Kim thought everyone saw like she did."

My Hilton Lions Club was doing an eye screening at our town's fall apple festival and my part was to do a screening for depth perception. I was a seventh-grade teacher at the time. One of my students came by and I invited her to try the test. Her mother was in the area and I asked her to do it also. My student Kim had gotten four out of ten correct. Her mother got correct ten out of ten. Neither of us nor Kim knew she had a vision problem. Kim thought everyone saw like she did. Her parents got her checked professionally and she was a very happy girl after that. That was when I realized how important it was that I was a Lion. (Lion James Schiebel)

"Sight projects giving people their lives back"

Ron and I, together, have worked with and for Lions for over ninety years. Ron realized his worth as a Lion when he took a little girl, who had very poor eyesight and was from a very poor family for her eye glasses. I became a true Lion one late night when I drove retrieved eyes from our hospital to our Lions Eye Bank Center. We knew all was worthwhile as we thought of a little girl able to learn in school and the possibility of two people who were now able to see because eyes had been donated. Sight projects continued in our Lion's lives as together we led as Sector Coordinators for Campaign SightFirst II and were certainly excited when the world raised over 200 million US dollars! At our fiftieth-wedding celebration we requested a donation to this campaign and were amazed when we were able to present four Melvin Jones Fellowships to deserving Lions! This was followed as LCIF District Coordinators visited all of the clubs in our district to promote our awesome International Foundation. Most recently we worked with Lions, our local School Board and the Ontario Optometrists Association to form a unique partnership in a special

EyeSee EyeLearn program for Junior Kindergarten students, providing some simple tests, promoting a free visit to an optometrist and they in turn providing the first glasses free when required. Where would our lives be without our Lions connection? (Lion Ron & Lion B. J. Finlay)

"Clean water for a desperate school"

As a member of Lions Club of Harare, The Phoenix, we had a twinning project with Lions Club Gold Coast Mermaids of Australia. The President Lion Keith Robinson and Lion Dianne came to Zimbabwe and identified a school which is about 250km from Harare called Zinatsa. This school is in a rural setting and there was no access to clean water for the children and the community. The kids had to travel several kilometers carrying containers to the nearest river and they would carry the drinking water back to their homes and also their school. The Lions in Australia assisted in raising money for a borehole to be drilled at the school. We as the Lions in Zimbabwe oversaw the project on the ground. Upon completion of the project, Lion Keith came down from Australia for the commissioning of the borehole and storage tanks. As we turned on the borehole for the first time and water started coming out of the taps, just the expressions on the faces of the village elders and the children from the village who had gathered told a humbling story that we had not just changed the lives of the school children, but that we had changed the lives of a community. I was so touched by this experience as I know we take a lot of things for granted and by being a Lion I had been able to be part of changing lives. Proud to be a Lion. (Lion Jona Machaya)

"I realized I could go beyond my neighborhood."

I was sitting at my local Lions Club meeting listening to an annual report of how our club had provided ten pairs of eyeglasses to people in need. In South Milwaukee, when people need eyeglasses and cannot afford them, we refer them to a local optician and then we pay for the eyeglasses one pair at a time. Our club is probably pretty similar to most other clubs in this regard. In 2004, we all felt good about providing assistance to the ten recipients. Then came my *aha!* moment. I went on a Wisconsin Lions Eye Mission to Mexico where we distributed 4,000 pairs of eyeglasses in one week to people who needed them. I remember one of the people I personally helped. He had come to get a replacement pair of eyeglasses for the pair he had broken eighteen years earlier. He was accompanied by his eighteen-year-old son; and when I put his glasses on him, he looked at his son ... whom he had never been able to clearly see. I will never forget that moment or the expression on his face because I realized that in Lions, I could go beyond my neighborhood to make a massive impact on the lives of people in the world. (Lion Karla Harris)

"The grant that saved a family"

There recently was a family in our town that lost their house in a fire. One of our members applied for a grant through Lions of Michigan and we got 1,000 US dollars to assist in replacing some of the items they still needed. Hearing how grateful the family was reminded me why I continue to serve. It was absolutely priceless! (11:5)

"Giving the children the future they deserve"

I have become a Zone Chair for our PediaVision program and also chairperson for our club. Using the Spot camera to check kids and adults for eye problems has become heartwarming. Through the use of this machine our club has caught several children with severe eye problems. It is extremely rewarding to be a part of preventative measures to help save these children from blindness as they get older. I feel as though I am helping to give them a future. (11:26)

"With the letter came a repayment."

My Lions Club helped a disadvantaged young man once with 500 Finnish Marks, so that he could actualize a study trip abroad. The young man later moved to the country he had studied in and established a good career there. Some twenty years later, he contacted us again to thank us for the help he received which had been a significant springboard to his career. With the letter came a repayment to our Club of 5000 Finnish Marks. (2:33)

"I saved a baby from lack of milk."

In support after the Great East Japan Earthquake, within ten days I delivered ten tons of relief supplies from Lions Clubs to the devastated area. What touched me the most from handing out the relief supplies to afflicted people was the moment I gave the powdered milk that was asked from the local member of Lions Club in the devastated area. I was proud of myself for saving a baby from lack of milk because the local officials only had a little amount of powder milk as a relief supply and the mother's milk did not come out from stress caused by shock of earthquake. I learned what is very important and needed when disaster occurs. (6:2)

"Our club helped the life of this kid."

In a health fair for a poor public school with kids in need, the director of the school came to us asking for help. One boy had a big bump in his head that look like a horn. This happened due to an accident when he was really young. The family was really poor and could never help the kid. Through contacts, we found doctors to remove this bump by surgery. Our club really helped the life of this kid. This will make a whole difference in his life! (8:70)

I Took Action

"These were the first medals that he had ever won."

In 2001–2002, when I was Service Activities Chairman for District

202G, I took on the role of Special Olympics Coordinator for the Sight First Opening Eyes Program. Our role was to meet the Special Olympians as they arrived in Auckland and get them to Logan Park where a team of optometrists and ophthalmologists were ready to test their eyes. Once tested, the Special Olympians with the assistance and guidance of Lions were able to choose eye glass frames that were sent away for the fitting of the lenses. We tested more than 800 Special Olympians and provided eye glasses to nearly half of those tested. Some required special glasses for the event in which they were competing. One young man arrived with his team and he was a bit of a character. I spoke to his caregiver and she said that his sport was swimming. Andrew had attended a number of Olympics but had never won a medal as he always got tangled up in the lane ropes. After having his eyes tested, the ophthalmologists decided to have made for him some every day glasses and some swimming goggles. He was fitted with his special swimming goggles before he left us. I was invited to attend the Special Olympics Opening Ceremony and was blown away when Andrew was seen marching in with his team still wearing his swimming goggles. These he wore the entire day and his caregiver informed us he had even worn them to bed. I did not see Andrew again until the day of the closing ceremony. We were once again invited to attend the function. There at the medal presentations was a very excited Andrew, and around his neck were four gold and three silver medals. These were the first medals that Andrew had ever won. That my friends was the day I knew I had become a LION. (Lion Eric Carter)

"I saw the joy on the child's face."

I was stationed in Korea during the war. It was near Osan that I had an experience that would affect my life forever. I saw children heading south. They didn't have much for clothing. They were dirty and forced to look after themselves. I saw them digging in the mud to carve out a spot where they could draw heat from the earth and sleep. Outside of our quarters we had garbage cans and after they thought all of the soldiers were gone, the children would creep in and find whatever they

could from what we had thrown away. It was terribly sad. It wasn't long after I returned from Korea about a year before the war was over that I went to visit a gas station owner that I had worked for while attending college. I worked two nights a week pumping gas while I was in college to help make ends meet. The owner of the station was glad to see me and he said he wouldn't take no for an answer. He was taking me to dinner. It turns out, the dinner was a Lions Club meeting and the District Governor was the program speaker. He had prepared thirty-five mm color slides on corneal transplants and how Lions helped transport the corneal tissue across the state to world-renowned WillsEye Hospital in Philadelphia where cornea transplant surgeries were performed. I saw what Lions were doing for people; and one of the slides showed a child who had received the surgery and when the bandages were removed I saw the joy on his face. That slide had an effect on me; it reminded me of the children I had seen in Korea. That image of joy struck everyone at the meeting the same way. I was so impressed about what Lions were doing; and when I was asked to join I immediately accepted. (Lion Joseph Wroblewski)

"The milk was spilt and the bottles were broken."

I was invited to join a Lions Club by my business partner as a young man. He paid my entrance fee for me and I became an active Lion becoming a club president, district governor, international director, DGE group leader, and a ten-time board appointee, before becoming an executive officer. Thinking back, at the age of thirty-one, I started my own business. I was fortunate to have a successful company. One day, when I looked out onto a side street I saw a young kid riding a bicycle on the street. He was delivering 300 bottles of milk. The street was rough and he hit a bump and fell off the bike. All of the milk was spilt and the bottles were broken. I gathered my staff together and we went outside to help him clean it up. He looked so poor and upset about what had happened. I asked him how much he had lost and he said 300 dollars. At that time, a monthly salary in Korea was about sixty dollars. So, I thought about what Lions had done for me and I gave him 300 dollars to cover his loss. He was overwhelmed and didn't know what to say. He told me that he would repay me just as soon as he could. But I told him that wasn't necessary and he didn't have to repay me; he should use his resources to help someone else in the future when a similar misfortune happens to them. (Lion Jung-Yul Choi)

"A baby born in a prison corridor"

A baby born in an unhygienic prison corridor. A lady born with a passion to love. A gentleman born with a heart to serve. On the twenty-eighth of August 2015, a twenty-three-year-old mother gave birth to her third baby in an extremely unhygienic prison corridor in Negombo, Sri Lanka. The prison holding over one hundred female inmates had only a shrine room to examine the patients and a table with a huge hole in the middle. The moment I found out about this tragedy I was determined to build a medical ward for the prisoners. I searched for donors around the world. Most Sri Lankans believe that prisoners should suffer for their sins, therefore, attempts to raise funds were met with hostility. As months rolled by I felt alone, abandoned and misunderstood, but my faith in God strengthened me. My love for my sisters behind bars kept me going. On the 18th of November 2015, I met the president of the Lions club of Inner Colombo, Lion Gopihran Shanmuganathan who is a building constructor. When I told him about my desire to build a medical ward for the female prisoners he caught onto the vision and immediately volunteered not only to build but to furnish and equip the medical ward. My dream became a reality! It's a miracle and Lions can do miracles; they are everyday heroes. On the tenth day of April 2016, the prison medical ward was declared open by our District Governor Christy Nanayakara. (Lion K S P Dharminie Fernando)

"Filling hungry stomachs"

One day I walked out of my neighborhood Hindu temple after prayer. I saw a poor, hungry beggar outside. I gave a coin and left. I saw this beggar again a few days later, this time he was sitting outside a mosque. I was confused. I asked the beggar, "Are you a Hindu or a Muslim?" He replied, "I am hungry." In that moment many decades ago, I realized that I am a Lion. I am neither Hindu nor Muslim. I am someone who fills hungry stomachs. (Lion Naresh Aggarwal)

"Defying the expected"

When I was still a Leo, I found out about an extremely gifted young boy whose guardians could not pay for the specialized education he needed to reach his full potential. We as Leos, took it upon ourselves to raise funds for him to have a uniform, books, and cover the unexpected costs. The funding continued from the Lions Club through high school and college. He is now a well-educated young man with a degree and his life is exponentially different than was predicted for someone in his situation. I hope he is living his life to the absolute fullest every single day. (11:74)

"Today he has sight."

As the Charter President for my Crescent Bay Lions Club we were contacted by a young mother and father to see if we could help their new born blind baby. We said yes and within the first year he had two surgeries and today he has sight. We all are still very proud of what we had done for this family and young boy. (Lion Don Shove)

"Vision Honduras"

While in Honduras working on a Lions building project, I met a young lady carrying her Bible on the way to a church service. She asked if she could borrow my glasses so that she might be able to read it. The encounter prompted me to purchase her reading glasses which inspired the conception of *Vision Honduras*, a team of volunteers that provides eye glasses to people in need in Honduras and this continues to be our mission. (11:19)

"A family's peace of mind"

The Lions Club I belong to sponsors diabetic service dogs. We provide funds for a family with a diabetic child to pay for food, visits to the vet, and the many unexpected costs of owning a dog. Because I helped, this family has a service dog for their son. They are able to sleep through the night for the first time in eleven years because they know their service dog will alert them before something bad happens to their son giving them ample time to respond. This family's peace of mind will help them all grow closer to each other and make their lives a little bit easier in the midst of an undesirable, and at times life-threating, situation. I am honored to have been a part of this solution for them. (11:40)

"Every time we were emotionally moved."

My Club was involved with *Send the Light* to help the poor cataract patients to restore their eyesight. We not only supported them with money but also by surgery. Every time, we were emotionally moved when we saw they could see again. This feeling was stronger when we saw they could have better life. Hoaxing is the Guangdong Lion Club and we already have served around 600 people from June, 2004, in different places like Benching, Haji, Yanjing, and other cities in Guangdong. Hoaxing is a group that specifically serves the teenagers who live in poor areas with only grandparents. We cooperated with other Lion clubs and have served 430 students in Qiaojiao, Guangdong, giving 1000 yuan to each student every year for three years. This sponsorship was very much appreciated by the government and those working with these young people. (1:8)

"The outpouring of gratitude was beyond prediction."

Our Lions Club would visit nursing homes from time to time, singing and playing instruments. There was no need looking beyond those elderly people in the eyes to know if it made a difference or not. Aside from Lion events, my dad had become demented in a hospital. We went with my son (at the time, twelve years old) with instruments to the Christmas party. We accompanied group songs and performed a few Christmas songs together. I will remember my father's teary eyes forever of course but the outpouring of gratitude from the other patients, and above all the staff was beyond prediction. My father died half a year after that but my Christmas party in that hospital has continued. (2:24)

"I get emotional every time a blind person receives back his sight."

For me and for many others being a true Lion is the recognition that our service will help many people. I'm the president of the Lions Eye Bank and I get emotional every time I have the news that a blind person—thanks to the graft of corneal tissue from our bank—has received back his sight. (5:20)

"By helping others, we can feel good about ourselves."

I have been a Lion since 1979, always helping those in need with material and emotional support like visiting retirement homes. When we are there, we can see those elderly that were left behind by their children who never come to visit them. They need love, and that is when I love to volunteer. They tell me that they wish they had a daughter like me. Someone to bring them happiness. It's gratifying to see that your actions helped others become happier. Last year, we had a flood at Praia da Lago dos Patos–in Sao Lorenco do Sul–RS and I traveled all the way from Ganibaldi to help. I helped by registering everyone that lost their homes. I also helped by providing food, water, and shelter. These actions that we do for others give me the certainty that by helping others we can feel good about ourselves. (8:51)

"This is the happiest day of my life."

My Lions Club provided service for the municipal school, *Vitor*

Meireles, to test those having problems reading. While there, I noticed a child couldn't read the words easily. After the test, I talked to her mother to understand the situation. The mother was aware of the problems; however, due to low income she could never afford a pair of glasses. The child would always ask to sit in front of the class and would ask the teacher every time what was written on the board because of course she couldn't read. We took her and ten other children with similar problems and we gave them brand new pairs of glasses. When her child received the glasses, she took a deep breath and said, "this is the happiest day of my life because from now on I will be able to read the board without problems, and won't suffer headaches from trying to read the letters." This for me was gratifying! (8:83)

Intangible Gift

"The joy of a four-year-old and Santa"

All my life I saw my father Wallen who is a Past District Governor, heading to his Lions meetings, spearheading fundraisers, and volunteering at multiple fundraising events. I saw all of the fun he and my mother had with other Lions from as close as our neighborhood to as far away as South Africa! Of course, I couldn't wait to become a Lion and begin serving! Shortly after becoming a Lion I got married and that followed closely with having my beautiful daughter. My new little family was involved in everything that our club had to offer. At the annual Christmas celebration, we decorated a clubhouse in the community in preparation for Santa's arrival. During the event, the cutest young boy about four years old walked in. He was wearing an old winter jacket, boots, and sweats so thin there was no way he was warm enough on that cold winter day. He came running into the hall, turned to his left and saw Santa! With the biggest smile that only a child can have, he said, "Mom! It's Santa! It's Santa!!!" I stood there with tears in my eyes and love in my heart! Even to this day as I write this, it brings tears to my eyes that we were able to bring the joy of Santa to this little

Boy. As a Lion, I serve to make someone's day a little brighter and the world a better place! (Lion Jennifer Ware)

"Her name was Mary."

We had delivered food to nine of the ten families our club had adopted. One to go. We found the trailer on the edge of town. My buddy told me I could handle this one all by myself. He saw the two dogs before I did. Armed with a large box of food and a package of hotdogs if needed to distract the dogs, I made my way to the porch. When the lady opened the door, I was shocked to see that she had lost her hair. Chemo no doubt. Her name was Mary. She asked me to carry the box of food to the kitchen as it was too heavy for her. That's when I saw two small children sitting on a broken sofa watching a black and white TV. Mary thanked me for the food and asked if I had a few minutes to talk. Mary told me how her husband had abandoned her and their children because he couldn't watch her die of cancer. She asked me if her life had been a mistake. I can't remember all the conversation but I told her that her life was not a mistake and that God loved her and her children and the love and care she was giving to her children would shape their lives forever. Mary needed to know that someone cared and to reaffirm her life. I still remember Mary. I remember the day that my acronym for Lions—Loving Individuals Offering Needed Service—became a reality for me. (Lion Sid Scruggs III)

"Helping those who want to help"

As a health care professional, I started working as a volunteer with individuals needing care in the 1970's at the height of the AIDS epidemic. I expanded that work by joining the City of Edinburgh Lions Club in 2009. I met a friend who was in Lions and who for many years nagged me to become a Lion. Knowing the individual had health issues but wanted to remain in Lions, I decided I would support him so he might continue his service. This made a difference to his life and together we became involved in supporting and encouraging disadvantaged and disabled members to join the organization. I have seen a difference in members' lives who feel valued for the work and service they do for Lions Clubs International. In particular, a young woman through her education at the Edinburgh Girls School in Malawi, Africa. Working together, serving others and expanding this to clubs in Argentina, Italy, Austria and Africa, gave the members greater understanding of other cultures and enormous confidence in themselves. One of my proudest moments as Club President was winning the Volunteer of the Year Award, given annually by the City of Edinburgh for our work in the local community and internationally. I went on to become a District Governor, lucky enough to witness and be involved in some amazing service projects across District 105NE and internationally. (Lion Andrew Kerr Sutherland)

"A wealth more valuable than any amount of money"

In central Pennsylvania, tradition has it that a New Year's Day dinner of pork and sauerkraut brings blessings and wealth. I joined the local Lions Club in 1999, but it wasn't until several years later that I had my *aha!* moment and came to truly understand what it meant to serve others. I was participating in our club's annual free New Year's Day Dinner project to our community. As I served residents their meals, I struck up a conversation with an elderly lady. As we chatted, she told me that if it weren't for the Lions she would have been alone at home eating a peanut butter and jelly sandwich. That conversation brought joy to my heart and still brings tears to my eyes. On that particular New Year's Day, along with a dinner of pork and sauerkraut and a very heart-warming conversation, I received blessings and a "wealth" beyond. That is the day I truly became a Lion! (Lion Kathy Fouse)

"I serve the world."

A group from our Lions Club of Sun City-Huntley volunteered to help out at the Sparrow's Nest Resale Store in Woodstock, IL. This is an extension of Home of the Sparrow, an organization that helps homeless women and children. Afterwards, we went to a local restaurant for lunch wearing our purple shirts. A patron came up to me and said, "You're with the Lions Club! You save the world." I said, "no, we serve the world." He replied, "Well, thank you for your service." I felt proud to be a Lion. (Lion Pat Krebs)

"Seeing her daughter for the first time"

A person in a sight program showed a picture of a mother in Honduras that had just received surgery and was seeing her child for the first time. It brings me to tears thinking of not being able to see my children's beautiful faces. I am glad the Lions Club was able to make such a profound and necessary donation for this family. (11:49)

"When a trip to the grocery store is a monumental task"

It is no surprise that elderly people who reside in assisted living homes have restricted freedom and independence. A trip to the grocery store that might have been easy for them twenty years ago has now become a monumental task leaving them frustrated and reminded that their lives will never be the same. As a Lion, I get the opportunity to run their errands, take them to doctor's appointments, and assist them with odds and ends. Being a nurse for twenty-five years has given me the unique opportunity to better serve these individuals and help bring a sense of peace and independence to their lives and I love it every day. (11:32)

"Uniting a community"

Dr. John Joseph is the medic for the Lion Clinc of Texas which serves those in need. The clinic serves those who cannot afford medical care by making it available at little or no cost to the members of the community. He asked me to become part of the project by serving on the clinic's board as a liaison between the community and the clinic in order to get the word out about the help that was available. It was a great project for my Lions Club serving all members of the community and help keep it united and strong. (11:73)

"A mother who finally believes in Santa Claus"

I was a member of the first Lioness club here in District 1A—the club was second in the state and third in the international program. I had twenty-three years of perfect attendance and three children; I planned meetings very carefully. For a number of years, we adopted families from a local community center for the Christmas holidays. We had a family with three children and one parent. We bought toys, foods, and even small gifts for the mother. As we never met the families we adopted, when we received thank you cards from the kids along with a very special note from the mom which said, "A long time ago I stopped believing in Santa Claus but now I know that Santa really is the Mayfair Lioness Club." This is why I am still a Lion today! Now over forty years later, my husband and I spend time at the Community Center again and read stories with the kindergarteners ages five and six. What a trip that was, particularly when they came up and helped us read! Again, I am reminded why I became and will continue to be a Lion. (11:48)

"Honoring my wife"

My daughter Karen decided to become a volunteer at a girl's orphanage in India while she was a student at Penn State University. She later became a sponsor for two girls, providing them with basic necessities and resources for school. Watching my daughter make a difference in these innocent girls' lives inspired me to become a sponsor. After my wife passed about fifteen years ago I realized how fulfilling it is to help someone less fortunate than you are and I believe that helped me to honor my wife's life and work through my grief. (11:44)

"A film festival bringing communities together"

I am a part of a Lions Club that has a program providing some entertainment for handicapped and underprivileged children in our community. We have a large indigenous population and a fair number of handicapped children. Over two Saturdays in March and April, I help to provide four free film sessions each Saturday for these children. Approximately, we average a total attendance of 2,400 people. The comments given to me and the written notes thanking us for the project fill me with a sense of wellbeing that is rarely felt in this day and age. I am currently excitedly preparing for our thirty-fifth festival. (11:13)

"Say cheese!"

Our club was going to a local park to make a donation to a summer camp for blind kids and I was asked to take a picture for the local newspaper. I lined up the kids, our Lions, and the camp staff, and took the photos. One of the blind kids, Bobby, said, "I can take pictures, my dad lets me use his camera, can I take your picture?" So, I gave Bobby my speed graphic, told him how to release the shutter and stood with everyone. Bobby aimed the camera at us, yelled, "Say Cheese!" and took the shot. I developed the film and burst out laughing. Bobby's picture was great, except he cut off the top of everyone's' heads! That one event is when I became a Lion. (11:37)

"The health and wellbeing of young women"

I assisted my group as we conducted menstrual hygiene awareness programs in more than twenty schools across the state. One school was for the deaf and I had to have the teachers translate for us. These types of programs are essential to the health and wellbeing of every young woman but require sacrifice and a lot of resources. By participating in this program, I feel that I am helping to keep the young women safe and enable them to be well educated about their bodies and their health. (11:52)

"It made me proud to be there."

I became a Lion in my heart the day I carried the flag at the international convention. It made me proud to be there and to be just part of such a wonderful event. I guess I've always felt like a Lion, but in my heart, I became one at that convention. (Lion Barb Becker)

"Raising morale and dignity"

As a Lion, I delivered meals to the elderly in Houston, Texas. These folks were shut indoors, limited by their restricted mobility and low morale. Visiting these people and providing them with a dignified meal and a smiling face was not only rewarding but an essential part of my own happiness. Often times the elderly are forgotten in this country and to be able to reach out and offer some hope and light in their day was life changing. (11:6)

"There's a lot of work to do."

I have been a Lion for thirty-eight years, but I was a Lion for sixteen years before I became a real Lion. That happened at my first district Lions convention. I was president of my club for the second time. I didn't know much about Lions in my first term. The second time, I found out about zone meetings, about cabinet, and conventions. At my first convention in Kindersley, I was hooked. I've only missed one convention since 1986. I'm a shift worker, so I'd take holidays to save up days so I could go to conventions. I'll be a Lion forever and I hope that's a long time. There's a lot of work to do, and I love it. (Lion Dennis Becker)

"He said that mine was a familiar voice."

Our club's ongoing activity is a few brothers at a time reading aloud the newspaper and magazines for the visually impaired. In other words, we record the newspapers/magazines once a week to disks and then distribute the disks through the organization for the visually impaired to the houses of about the one hundred visually impaired people that live nearby; and they listen to the newspapers/magazines with their own Daisy players. I had read newspapers/magazines for the first time and the next week we went to visit my spouse's father in the home for the elderly. When my spouse's dad came out from the living room to greet us, he pointed out the Daisy player. Then he looked me in the eye, grabbed my hand firmly as a mark of gratitude, and said that mine was a familiar voice. Then, I was proud. (2:82)

Robert S. Littlefield

"His beaming eyes have stayed in my memories."

As a president of my Lions Club in 1991, for an afternoon break for Christmas in a center for orphan children I disguised myself into Santa Claus. I took a child into my arms and his beaming eyes have stayed in my memories since then. (3:28)

"It was for me a testing experience."

I participated in helping a woman who lived in France return to her home in order to die near her family in Algeria, as she was in her final stages of cancer. I succeeded with my Lions Club to greet her in the airport of Algiers and I accompanied her to her familial home in a medical ambulance with an intensive care physician and a nurse. It was for me a testing experience and confirmed my commitment to service. (3:36)

"It was upsetting to realize what they had been missing."

I became a Lion in my heart when one day, as we were visiting a center for elderly people with the other members of the Lions Club and I asked an old man if he often had visits. His response terrified me and motivated me. He told me: "not since the last time you came to see me." This man had no family anymore and he was abandoned in this center. Another time, I was carrying food to a school for disadvantaged children and seeing the happy sights and smiles of these children in front of fruit and cheese, it was upsetting to realize they had been missing all the good we were giving to them. (3:45)

"The emotion turned into a desire."

I have never forgotten the shock of my first medical consultations in the Bush in Senegal with disabled children and few men to heal, re-educate, and clothe them. The emotion turned into a desire to transfer my know-how and to find how to be useful for a small part of the suffering humanity, and to tell it to people so that they join me in my humanitarian commitment. (3:62)

"Then I met 'an angel' I did not believe existed."

I am a professional doctor and I could tell many stories of the lives of people who asked for help. One of the last stories in particular gave me great joy. I did my duty for her according to my knowledge and believe (even knowing that such attitude would have a negative impact on the part of my superiors) after a few months I received a simple letter thanking me with these words: "I walked in the dark not knowing where to go and who to turn to, then I met an Angel! I did not believe existed, yet they are among us!" This is the most beautiful gift that I have ever received. (5:58)

"My heart was full of joy."

In 2010, we brought a trunk with many pairs of indoor shoes for people known as the mountain tribe in northern Thailand. They usually do not wear shoes. We collected the shoes from children who had graduated from kindergarten and elementary school. We cleaned and washed them. After we arrived, people from the tribe were eagerly choosing the shoes. A mother and the daughter were trying on pink shoes and they looked full of joy. When I looked at that sight, I was full of a happiness that I never felt before. On our way to Thailand the trunk was so full that my fingers hurt a lot carrying it. On our way home, the trunk felt very light because we didn't have any shoes to carry. But in some ways my feelings were much heavier because my heart was full of joy. (6:5)

"This will bring back happiness to my heart."

One of my first service projects as a Lion occurred when I met with an old gentleman who was ninety-two years old. He couldn't move by himself without help. His family was really poor and couldn't provide him much, only the essentials. When we gave him a brand-new wheel chair, he used all his strength left to sit down by himself. His words were: "this will bring back happiness to my heart." I use this motto for my personal life. I always want to bring happiness to other people's hearts, and my heart otherwise is not worth it. (8:65)

"Something so simply can make people happy."

I became a Lion in my heart when we collected used glasses to give to people that needed them but could not afford them. This really touched my heart. Something so simple can make many people happy by being able to see well. (9:38)

Inspired to Serve

"Passing on life from one to another"

When I was a young doctor, I learned what it was to feel like a Lion in the true sense. I had the opportunity to work in an emergency room so was able to really see life and death on the front lines. I saw some patients who could have been saved if a transplant were available. At that time, transplants were not common in Japan; even kidney transplants. But when I learned that Lions were doing that kind of activity, I proposed that transplants could be performed as a Lions' project. I coordinated one case of a family who lost a member and I suggested they donate the kidney to another person so their loved one could live on after death. That gave hope to the grieving family and was a really valuable and meaningful activity for me. Kidney transplants provide the opportunity to relay life from one person who is losing life to someone who is given the chance to live on. This idea of passing on life is not really a doctor's mindset; so, Lions helped me to see how transplants could function that way—to pass on life from one to another. Lions made my professional life richer. Lions helped me see that there can be something beyond the here and now. That made me believe in Lionism; and then, I started to work harder to coordinate donor programs. This effort made my hospital well-known and attractive to young doctors; and made the quality of care in my hospital better. I owe something to Lions in that sense, as well. My success as a doctor is because of Lionism and has become my motivation in my busy life. I will always give of my time to serve in a leadership position, if there is an opportunity. (Lion Dr. Jitsuhiro Yamada)

"Happiness in the children's hospital"

I was taking a tour of the Children's Hospital. The tour started with an incredibly detailed explanation about how the kids were supported during their stay. After the introduction of the hospital, I viewed a demonstration of an interactive display of fish on a digital floor to promote interaction and socialization. At one point in the tour, a young boy enthusiastically challenged me to dance with him. I was so moved in that moment. I also saw a very young little boy being towed in a worm-shaped mobile wagon. He was being pulled by his father and helped by his older brother who was pushing the IV pole. They were happy as can be despite their unfortunate circumstances. (Lion Lewis Quinn)

"A school in dire need of assistance"

When I joined Lionism about twenty-one years ago, we went to present food items to Nkhatabay School of the Blind. Due to government neglect, they were in dire need of assistance. Although these blind students could not see the presentations and handshakes, I could clearly see their gratitude and happiness through their genuine and sincere smiles and facial expressions. When I saw this, I thought of my own children who could see and had everything in life. I was so touched in my heart that my life completely changed from that moment and I promised to commit myself to serve those in need. I also became aware that no matter how small your help may seem, it makes a lot of difference to those in need, making their life dignified and worth living. From that moment, I have never forgotten that day and I take every opportunity I have in my life to serve the less privileged. Lionism is part of my life now and I am very proud to be a Life member as well. (Lion Faisal Karim)

"I was given the gift of sight not once, but twice."

When I was first asked to become part of the Lions family, there was never a question to say yes and I immediately wrote the check for my husband to become a member. This was before ladies were allowed to be Lions. He didn't understand my quick response until I later explained to him that The Greater Tampa Lions Sight Fund purchased my glasses for me as a child due to an eye screening at my elementary school. Later in life with the advancement of medical eye surgeries, I had RK (Radial Keratotomy) performed on both of my eyes with much success. I was declared legally blind prior to this surgery. I never knew that trees had leaves or grass had blades because before my surgery they were both just color blobs. I have been given the gift of sight not once, but twice in my lifetime and it is with all my heart that I say "Thank You" my Knights of the Blind for giving me the vision I have today by doing what you do as Lions. My husband has since passed and his donated corneas were transplanted giving someone the opportunity to see, a Lion who kept on giving. It is my honor to say I have been a Lion since 1981 and help give children and adults the gift of sight like I was given so many years ago. (Lion Jacqueline "Jackie" Cameron)

"No earthquake can stop hope."

To pick one story out of my experience as a Lion certainly was a challenge. Having been a Lion for almost a quarter of a century, I have been touched by as many souls as the days that I have lived. Since becoming an ambassador for Campaign Sight First China Action in 1997, I along with other participants of the project frequented various remote and rural areas in mainland China and offered cataract surgeries to the villagers. I still remember vividly the impact it had on me when I saw the patient regaining their eyesight for the first time. The overwhelming joy and satisfaction that ran through my veins made me understand why I became a Lion and realize how privileged I am to be able to get involved in this project. A week after the May 12 earthquake in Sichuan, a team of us travelled to the affected areas with medication and emergency supplies and visited the hospital where the survivors were treated. Amongst many, I remember Yang Liu lying in her hospital bed on her sixteenth birthday. Her double amputation left her so devastated she could not speak to us. Wang Li, another school girl we visited after the earthquake was busy preparing for her upcoming final examination. Even after losing her leg in the earthquake, she was so inspired by the kindness from everyone that she wanted to work even harder and so one day she can reciprocate. Most encouragingly, Yang Liu is now a painter and Wang Li got married last year with her lovely husband whom adores her tenacity and courage. I wish them all the best in life and I am most honored to be able to call these two beautiful young ladies my friends. (Lion Teresa Mann)

"They were prisoners."

There had been a major disaster. Lions Clubs had been challenged to conduct a fund raiser to provide relief for the victims of that event. The New England Lions Club decided to hold a Burgers in the Park event. The State Women's Correctional Center is in New England housing more than one hundred minimum, medium, and maximum security prisoners. The administrator was a member of the Lions Club and typically before the weekly Burgers in the Park, he would bring a small group of prisoners who were part of an outside work detail to the park to rake the lawn and clean the tables and picnic shelter. They were there that Saturday morning and they were puzzled. They asked why they were there then instead of on Tuesday afternoon. The prison administrator explained that the Lions were holding a fundraiser for the disaster victims. Later during the event, his cell phone rang. It was the prison with an order. The inmates had gathered the money for ninety-two meals. Now I was puzzled. The prison had a reputation for having one of the best kitchens among the institutions in the state. The inmates had little or no money to spend. Some of them with good behavior might work in the prison's industries for a few dollars. With little money to spend and certainly a much better meal within the prison than our burgers, I asked why they would do this. He responded, "They don't often have an opportunity to help those less fortunate than themselves." They were prisoners. (Lion Lewellyn Rustan)

"Gretta's strength"

The day I met Gretta. It all began in 1996 (twenty years ago) when I was District Governor. I was invited to Richmond Club (2015 Sydney) to present some Melvin Jones Fellowships by the President Dianne Sherrington. Whilst sitting at the head table, I noticed a young girl (six years old) come into the room in a wheel chair. She was taken out of the wheel chair and placed in a walking frame that allowed her to stand upright and with the aid of pulleys attached to her shoes, she was able to walk. From a wheel chair to walking. The President told me the club had paid for her to go to England to be fitted with this special walker. I made some inquiries the next day to the organization that was going to import the walkers. I asked, "how much do you want?" I was told 300,000 dollars. So, we set to work and raised the money in twelve months to commence the program. The program we donated the money to is called the Australian Lions Children's Mobility Foundation. I witnessed many emotional moments as children stood for their first time. Now over 1,000 children can walk and experience the feeling of being upright and gain independence. This has had a huge impact on all the families. Now twenty-six years old, Gretta who used to only be able to speak through her computer, is now a University student and very independent young woman. It was a very emotional moment to see her again after twenty years. The final act was for me to induct her into Lions. (Lion Barry Palmer)

"Student sobriety"

My Lions journey began in 1962 when I became a member of the Watford City, North Dakota, (USA) Lions Club. I took an active part in club activities and after a few years became club president. In 1975, I moved with my family to Bismarck, North Dakota, where I joined the Bismarck Lions Club. Although I became a member of Lions in 1962 it wasn't until 1986 that I became a Lion. My awakening came when I attended the North Dakota State Lions Convention in Williston. The convention program included a session sponsored by Lions Quest which dealt with helping troubled youth who were fighting alcohol and drug addiction. There were twelve high school students who gave testimonies about their various experiences as they worked to become sober students once again. There was high emotion with tears being shed, especially by the members of the large audience. I did not know and could not believe that the Lions organization was involved in programs such as this. The Lions were not only saving troubled youth but were also saving lives. I was astounded. It was while driving home from that convention that I made a decision to become more involved in the work of Lions. As a result, I become a district governor in 1991–1992 and an International Director in 2002–2004, positions which allowed me to have much greater impact on the mission of Lions Clubs International. (Lion Bruce Schwartz)

"Overcoming barriers to become first female District Governor"

Sometime in January 2005, during my morning break at Serowe College of Education in Botswana where I was a Department Head, a very good colleague invited me to attend a meeting that evening. He was sure that I would be interested in going because he saw me as a people's person. I attended and was very much impressed by the professional manner in which it was conducted. I attended two consecutive meetings. During this period, I attended a number of service activities including health camps, feeding the elderly, distributing clothing, and providing for disaster victims. Then I was contemplating whether I would be able to cope with the demands of joining such a club. I started asking myself: would I not need a car? Where would I get sufficient funds to move around? How am I going to balance my work and the activities of the club? Then suddenly it dawned on me that here I was along with others who were finding time to assist persons within that community who were less privileged than myself. Then I thought, hey, I am from a family of twelve–six girls and six boys–and my father was the sole breadwinner. I am quite sure there were many persons who were assisting my parents so why not do the same for others? So, in May 2005 I decided to become a member of Lions Club International. To my surprise, I even ended up as my district's first female DG! (Lion Frances Margaret Palmer)

"LCIF Inspired me."

One month after joining Lions, *The LION* magazine carried a story on Campaign SightFirst I. I was so impressed; I knew I wanted to be a part of that. LCIF has been at the root of my enthusiasm for almost twenty-five years now and I am so impressed with all of the programs emanating from this organization. They really hit at the core of my interests, feelings, and concerns. (Lion Donald R. Hieb)

"Lions club paid for my education; now I'm paying it forward."

As a young man who grew up in the rural area of Blantyre District, Chileka in Malawi and raised from a humble family that survived on subsistence farming, I had never heard about the Lions Club. In 1970 I was one of the students selected from Blantyre to receive a school grant from Blantyre Lions Club after obtaining the highest score during the primary school leaving certificate exams. Thirty-five years later in 2005, I was invited to a Lions club meeting and never connected it until I had attended several meetings. Once I realized this was the organization that paid for my secondary school fees for the first year, I resolved to join and serve other under privileged students and communities. Since I was inducted on August 8, 2005, I have developed into a devoted Lion serving my club, region, and District 412. My commitment to my club in the fundraising of resources to finance club projects in education, health, environment, and youth development has inspired my active involvement and now I am one of the faculty team members (as an FDI graduate) training and inspiring new Lions to become better servants of a world begging for good leadership. (Lion Ken Banda)

"Five-year-old Wendy standing tall"

I had experienced many good deeds of Lionism since accepting a membership in the Conception Bay Lion Club in 1973 that supported my positive feelings toward our motto, *We Serve!* However, it was the year that

I had served as governor (1985–1986) that consolidated my thoughts of being a Lion forever. When I had witnessed the solid commitment by our Lions and Lionesses to our very own Lion Max Simms Memorial Camp for the handicapped in a united effort to make sure that all handicapped locals in Newfoundland and Labrador would have the opportunity to receive an enriching and rewarding camping experience, I bowed to the feeling of devotion. In that same year, I dedicated myself as a permanent Lion when I stood tall with the giants of the Lions District to support the Norman's Cove Lions Club Wendy Thorne Project. Twenty-four ladies, many of them Lionesses of Norman's Cove, volunteered to go to the home of Wendy, a five-year-old, stricken with cerebral palsy for four hours a day, six days a week to help in the implementation of a physical developmental program in conjunction with the rehabilitation center in St. John's. After six trips going to Toronto's children's hospital and dozens of trips to the rehabilitation center, Wendy had shown improvement. Her beautiful smile tugged gently at my heart strings. This had truly been my focal point, fusing my thoughts on vision and passion for future services in Lionism. (Lion Cecil Parsons)

"What matters most"

I would have to say that I became a Lion on the second disaster I ever assisted on; the F5 Tornado in Oklahoma. Standing next to a family who was looking at a blank slab that was once their house and everything they owned, I helped them realize that they still had each other and that the things could be replaced. With the help of Lions Club, I was able to assist them in replacing the things they had lost. (11:34)

"Housing projects and natural disasters"

My wife is from Tacloban, Philippines, so when the typhoon, Haiyan, hit that area and destroyed the lives of the people living there it struck a deep chord in me and I had to do something. Within minutes I was on the phone raising money for relief efforts provided by LCIF. After two weeks of fundraising, we were able to send 15,000 Euros to provide resources to the people affected by this catastrophe. When I went there to visit and see the progress they were making, it was especially rewarding to be able to see the six housing projects our funds went towards. (11:28)

"Always remember the ones who are hungry."

One year we were handing out food baskets to families and children in the community and we were greeted with tears of joy and immense gratitude. Something we take for granted every day. Food. To see the surprise and beautiful gratitude in these peoples' faces reminded me how important it is to not get caught up in the mundane activities of life, rather look back and always remember the ones who are hungry. (11:8)

"It's the first time people have asked nothing in return."

I was president of the club in 2004–2005. My club organized an action for the back to school, aiming at 732 schoolboys and girls coming from six different schools that are located more than 300 km (130 miles) from the capital city. The aim was to reward the best girl students and then both boys and girls. In its intervention while awarding the prizes, one of the local official addressed the Lions Club saying "it is the first time people have come to honor us without asking for something in return. Usually, when benefactors come up to here, it's to give their offer in return of voting for them or a political party." This day I was really proud to belong to a wonderful association. (3:74)

"I will continue supporting them."

After the Great East Japan Earthquake, I felt that I was not doing anything except sending money to help. However, I was fortunately able to hold a networking event with Tamura Lions Club which is close to the Fukushima nuclear power plant. Small temporary housing had less support against the cold compared to the large temporary housing and the winter was coming soon. So, we sent electric blankets for the people who lived in the small temporary housing. Also, there was a problem for children in that the number of who were overweight increased because they went to school by bus every day they had little opportunity for physical education. Even though many houses have been reconstructed, still more than half of the students live in the temporary housing. I will continue supporting them. (6:34)

"Because we are Lions"

It was 2011 and the EF5 tornado hit Joplin, Missouri. I was watching the television and knew I had to do something. I looked at my wife, and she looked at me. I did this a few times and finally she said "you need to go to help in Joplin." I got my truck ready and four days later, I was on my way. When my community learned what I was about to do, they all wanted to get involved. The local quilt shop donated a quilt. I decided to use it as a fundraiser and told people they could sign the quilt for a donation. People signed … and I brought 1,500 US dollars with me to donate to the Joplin community. The food pantry contacted me and donated one ton of food. I only had a three-quarter ton truck, so the food pantry coordinators lent me a trailer so I could bring it all to Joplin. As I was leaving, my little granddaughter wrote something on the center panel of the quilt that touched my heart and reminded me why I will always be a Lion. Her words: "Love is on the way!" When I got to the Joplin Host Lions Club meeting to present them with the food and check, the District Governor Debbie Cantrell just looked at me and cried: "Why are you doing this for us? You came from so far away, and didn't even know us." I knew in my heart the reason. I answered, "Because we're Lions, Debbie. We're all as one." (Lion Jim Groff)

"Mr. Al, I want to be a Lion"

District Governor Al Funk and I were driving together to the District meeting. I asked Al when he had realized how critically important Lions are in the lives of so many people. Al looked at me and said, "I really didn't become a Lion until last year." Then, he told me the story. He received a call one day from Make-A-Wish Foundation about a young boy who had chosen to go to Hawaii for his last wish before he died. Right before he was scheduled to leave, he went into the hospital. When he came out, he had had a birthday and was now over the age of twenty-one. Make-A-Wish cannot accept anyone who is over the age of twenty-one. Make-A-Wish Foundation called Al and asked whether the Lions could raise the money to send Joey to Hawaii. Al's response was, of course the Lions could raise the money; and Al did raise the money. Again, Joey was scheduled to leave; and again, he had to return to the hospital. This time when he came out, he needed an additional nurse to accompany him on the trip. Again, the money was raised. The trip began. Al said, "I guess the mistake I made, if it was a mistake, was being at the airport when Joey returned. I saw Joey and I asked him how his trip was and his response was Oh, Mr. Al, it was wonderful." And then Al said, "What do you want to do now, Joey?" To Al's great surprise, Joey said, "Mr. Al, I want to be a Lion." "Joey, we would love to have you become a member of our Lions club." Joey became a member and went to the meetings every week for the next eleven months before he died. Al said it was the hardest thing to see Joey in his casket. Al said, with tears in his eyes, "I became a Lion the moment I looked down in that casket and I saw what Joey's last wish was. His last wish was to be buried in his Lions vest." (Lion William L. "Bill" Biggs)

"Dad, there's a step there."

I was asked to join my local Lions Club in January; and was elected President in March. I had no clue what Lions was about so I went online to learn what I could. One of the things I found out was that I was supposed to go to conventions. That year, the district Lions convention was in Weyburn, so I went. The convention had many interesting programs, but one of them stuck in my mind. There were some local residents talking about Scotopic Sensitivity Syndrome, a problem with the brain's ability to process visual information. This problem tends to run in families. Those affected are bothered by the glare of florescent or bright lights, sunlight, and sometimes lights at night. Individuals with this vision problem may have problems focusing on or distinguishing letters, words may be inverted or in columns and depth perception is also a problem with this vision problem. The Weyburn Lions Club was providing assistance to a little girl because she needed specially-colored lenses to help her overcome the syndrome. The father of the girl told a story that provided my *aha!* moment. He said that for twelve years, his daughter tripped every day when she opened the front door to step up into the house. Every day she tripped. Then, the family learned about the special lenses and they took her to get the glasses. When she got home, she opened the door and didn't trip. She said, "Dad, there's a step there." She had tripped for twelve years because she couldn't differentiate between heights. Lions made a total difference in her life and I realized then what being a Lion was all about: Making a difference in people's lives. (Lion Rob Hill)

Conclusion

English author, Rudyard Kipling was known to say that if history were taught in the form of stories, it would never be forgotten. The one hundred memorable stories included in this chapter provided a snapshot of the millions of special moments explaining why Lions throughout the one hundred years of their history as an association have dedicated their lives to serving those in need. Stories provide a picture into the hearts of the tellers; and these stories revealed how the experiences, personal realizations, individual and collective actions, intangible gifts, and inspirational moments motivated them to hear and respond to the call of service. In chapter 6, empathy is introduced as a state of mind that enhances the commitment to service for a lifetime.

Lions Club of the University District at Theodora Home 1930

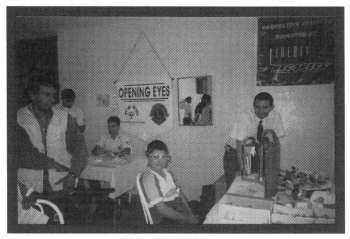

Lions distribute glasses to boys at Opening Eyes
Program, Michigan Special Olympics 1995-2005

Chapter 6

Confirming the Call to Serve

"To be able to give back to the community that is my home makes my efforts a very personal experience. To have the Lions team working side by side and to see real differences from your efforts makes for a community that is closer, rather than drifting apart as seems to be the norm in society these days. I have gained friendships, personal growth, and social awareness well above my expectations. This is why I will always continue to be a Lion!" (11:12)

Stories are at the core of this book about the service from the heart. These stories and personal reflections have revealed the variety of service experiences and what they have meant to the individuals who identified service to others as an essential part of their lives. Stories contribute to the construction of reality and provide a way of looking at the world, reflecting the beliefs, desires, and values of the storytellers (Bruner, 1991). Lions look at the world through the eyes of empathy and with a sincere desire to raise people up from their personal challenges through service.

Stories are personal and not meant to be generalized beyond the experiences of the teller; and yet, the stories in this book come together in a special way to tie the experiences of volunteers into a framework that appears more universal than what might have been otherwise thought possible. We arrived at this point of summary by establishing an historic foundation from which service opportunities were encouraged and facilitated. Over the past one hundred years, LCI enabled organized service activities to expand their impact in unique ways. The stages of expansion started with creative ways to make the fledging organization stand out and appeal to the those who would become the first Lions accepting the call to service. As challenges confronted LCI during the survival stage, local Lions Clubs accepted the directional approach offered by the leadership of the association and focused their service on particular areas of need; for example, youth, vision, and community causes. As the organization matured and expanded worldwide, Lions recognized needs around the globe and established a more coordinated approach to service to promote consistency and a collective adherence to a common vision for the future. Specific programs initiated new opportunities for greater impact through the Lions Clubs International Foundation. At the start of its second century of service, LCI has renewed itself through the strategic planning process— LCI Forward—with service platforms enabling volunteers to find new ways to respond to the established and ever-growing needs around them.

Naturally, over the past one hundred years, people were attracted to service based upon number of reasons, ranging from a belief that service was part of their personal identity to their motivation to make the world a better place. But, in order to sustain service, a match was essential between the act of service and how it functioned for the volunteer to fulfill a motivational need. The intersection of a meaningful service activity with the ongoing commitment to service produced stories from the heart. For these participants, initial motivation may have been prompted by something other than what they later acknowledged to have solidified their commitment to service; a time when they believed they became Lions *in their hearts*.

This confirmation process was needed for the long-term adoption of this new and innovative way of thinking about serving the needs of others. Sociologist Everett Rogers (2003) found that an individual decision to adopt a new behavior was not enough to prolong its adoption. In order to sustain the ongoing commitment to behave in a particular way, the individual must confirm the decision through experience or observation. As we know, people have joined Lions Clubs for a variety of reasons. But for those who have remained Lions, their experiences and observations confirmed their ongoing commitment to serve.

The one hundred stories included in chapter 5 shared the service experiences that changed the lives of the tellers. The stories were personal. But, there was something else. These stories offered a glimpse into the hearts of the volunteers and showed their vulnerability and sensitivity to those around them. In these stories, you saw people who became closely involved with each other. The receivers of service exposed their vulnerability by asking for or seeking help; the givers of service exposed their sensitivity and empathy through their willingness to make a commitment to help. The tellers exposed their empathy and concern for their fellow human beings.

Empathy is a complex concept that has been the subject of considerable study. William S. Howell (1982), a prominent communication scholar of the twentieth century provided insight into the definition of empathy that is helpful as we explore how Lions have confirmed their commitment to serve. Initially, empathy was considered as a physical response: "the tendency to imitate internally whatever held a person's attention" (p. 107). For example, early scientists noted that reactions and muscle movements were related to what people saw. Watching the pain experienced by others caused viewers to physically react.

Later, empathy was found to be more perceptual, as the person had a sensation of feeling what another was feeling. This is similar to putting yourself in someone's shoes. Howell expanded on this by suggesting that empathy was actually the ability to replicate what one perceived: "Just as a person possesses a language to the extent that he or she can speak it, so a person possesses empathy to the degree that empathetic response capability exists" (p. 107). This means that the observer not only views the physical tensions, but also the pain itself.

Think of a speaker who relates an extraordinary example of Lions' service that brings tears to the eyes of an entire audience as well as to the storyteller. As long as the observer perceives the need that is revealed in an example, for that observer the need exists and empathy is generated. The phrase, "where there's a need, there's a Lion," underlines not only the feeling and perception of the need by the Lion, but the capacity for that Lion to empathize and respond through service.

In reality, the stories in chapter 5 affirmed the qualities of a culture of Lionism built over one hundred years of volunteering and followed the advice of LCI founder, Melvin Jones: You can't get very far until you start doing something for someone else. The culture of Lionism was revealed time and time again through expressions and contact without the need for words of explanation; by the demonstration of helpfulness and a positive intent built upon a relationship forged through expressions of vulnerability and a willingness to help without knowing the individuals receiving the service; and a worldview based upon the commitment to take action and enact positive change in the world through servant leadership.

The first group of stories in chapter 5 identified meaningful experiences as evidence of the impact of service on the lives of the volunteers. These stories were associated with well-established priorities and reflected the history of LCI focusing on vision, hunger, youth, and the environment. Some of the stories identified going on mission trips, making surgery accessible to those in need, and conducting vision screening. Delivering food to families in need, baking cookies, and hosting a barbecue for physically challenged were stories associated with confronting hunger. Offering experiences—involving youth and provided for youth—included special needs camps, constructing schools, and volunteering at elementary schools. Even planting a community garden and helping victims of a flood demonstrated how focusing on the environment provided meaningful service opportunities.

The second group of stories illustrated how service made a difference, one life at a time. Helping a boy to succeed by paying 90 percent of the cost for his vision therapy, making it possible for deaf children to hear their mother's voice with hearing devices, and removing a deforming growth to normalize childhood experiences represented powerful examples of how individual Lions and clubs changed the lives of those in need. For some, restoring sight meant that a successful career would be possible for the recipient of the service. In other cases, developing a stronger personal commitment to the cause of Lionism was evidence that service changed the life of not only the recipient, but the giver of service.

The next grouping of stories gave evidence of the capacity of the volunteers to provide the service. In other words, having the agency or power to take action and do something provided a strong narrative for a commitment to service. The storytellers assumed new roles, joined clubs, paid it forward, built and equipped medical wards, fed the hungry, gave glasses, provided security, supported students, improved vision, and built positive feelings and self-confidence among the Lions who told them. Service was empowering and they recognized that power in their lives.

The intangible gifts of service as the fourth group were unmistakable as the stories unfolded. Some Lions felt valued and appreciated by the sick and diseased knowing someone cared; and others had a sense of wellbeing after the service was performed. Expressions of joy and love were shared through tears, profound expressions of caring, and happiness. The words in the stories conveyed the tenderness felt by the volunteers as they looked into beaming eyes of children and were equated with the angels for the services they were performing.

Finally, some of the stories shared the inspiration felt by the givers of service and how their lives were changed. Many testimonies shared insight about developing a stronger commitment to service, making one's professional life richer, and realizing what Lions can do together. Being humbled by the desire of a dying young man to become a Lion or by the willingness of prisoners to help disaster victims through their donations was inspiring. Responding to the tornado victims in Joplin, Missouri, USA without even knowing them or serving the needs of victims of disaster in the Philippines or Botswana and asking nothing in return revealed the inspiration felt by the storytellers.

As a whole, the power of these stories creates a history for service for Lions around the world. American psychologist Jerome Bruner suggested that, "narratives accrue … and eventually create something variously called a 'culture' or a 'history' or, more loosely a 'tradition'" (1991, p. 18). The culture of rendering service as an obligation of membership in Lions Clubs International is an expectation that has guided its members to focus their efforts on the forgotten and those in need. While the history of the association has documented changes as challenges and new opportunities confronted its membership, the tradition of putting the welfare of others before self has produced countless stories with deep meaning for the tellers.

That's where we are today. Over the past four years, Lions have been celebrating the past and planning for the future led by four International Presidents spanning five International Boards of Directors. Planting the seeds of renewal, President Joe Preston launched the LCI Forward initiative that culminated with the identification of the new concept of service platforms during the term of Dr. Jitsuhiro Yamada. Sharing the centennial year of 2017 in their respective terms of office as International Presidents, Chancellor Bob Corlew first encouraged Lions to expand the impact of Lionism as they climbed new mountains of service and then handed off the second century to Dr. Naresh Aggarwal to inspire Lions to integrate the

Power of We, the *Power of Service*, and the *Power of Action*. The question remains, what more can we learn from the responses of those who have made a commitment to prolonged service?

Final Thoughts from the Survey Participants

In 1917, Lions Clubs International was born; and today Lions continue to have the opportunity and obligation to recommit to service as a life-changing experience. The final question on the survey asked the respondents: Is there anything else you would like to share about your volunteer experience that keeps you motivated to give more of your time to serving the needs of others? In their responses, 585 provided additional comments, many of which expanded their earlier reflections. However, two additional themes emerged that were especially meaningful to the participants: Belonging to a Lions Club enhanced the service experience; and the perceived connection between service and a higher spiritual power.

The following sampling of responses reveals the connection felt by participants towards membership in a Lions Club and their ongoing commitment to service: "Together with my friends from Lions I feel like we are doing something meaningful" (9:10); "Being a Lion has given me the opportunity to learn from other Lions the best way to overcome obstacles and to keep focus on my objectives in life, business and family while helping others to gain a sense of security that others care about them and their lives" (11:46); "Volunteers are the happier and more cheerful people, because they are giving a little bit of themselves to others, they are not frustrated, because they live in community and are surrounded by people with the same goals" (8:35); "What we can do is to stimulate people to participate in groups that benefits people or the community" (8:57); "I believe I grew a lot once I joined Lions Club. Besides the numerous people that I have met and now I call them real friends, I was able to develop my leadership skills, that I didn't even know I had" (8:71); "My experience is happiness from serving, seeing my children volunteering and loving what they do, and understanding that life can be challenging, and it's better to give then to receive" (8:85); "A volunteer worker rarely can be a lone hard worker. The public image of a volunteer group is important. The image as a member of a good volunteer group makes you feel that your own image is good" (2:34); "It is important for me to participate in the club as a volunteer with enthusiasm, commitment, and responsibility. To dedicate a little part of your time to serve with love. It's like sharing feeling with your family making it one of the greatest feelings" (10:21); "The friendships/relationships you make with other Lions are very important. There are many more Lions in other countries that you can become friends with and to have fun with" (10:40); "At this moment in the world there is so much physical and psychological distress that everyone can certainly find some kind of appropriate way to lend a helping hand to someone in a worse position. At the beginning, a small impactful act grows by the help of a large group of people into more impactful and significant acts" (2:23); "Humanitarianism is not the only thing that has to be taken into account. We should not forget about culture, education, youth, respect of the environment. It is why Lionism is a combination of humanitarianism and humanism. It's what makes Lions Clubs unique and guarantees their future" (3:50); "Nowadays in the world we live in, where each individual is selfish, being part of a Lions Club, being a volunteer is a blessing" (8:13); "The motivation for my service is being part of a group, to work with the organization. There are always needs and there are always Lions to help solve that problems" (10:86); "Belonging to an organization such as LCI gives me the opportunity to reach beyond my small world to the larger world. It expands my knowledge of other people" (11:59); "I have been left a widower twice, the marriages were romantic and happy. My losses have been insurmountable. The last passing made me so numb that our president came to get me personally to come to the club night. I felt that a strong sense of belonging in our club had been instilled in me, I had been a founding member, there I had also been cared about. So, life continues and I give all my energy to those friends of mine" (2:47); and "Everyone should have the opportunity to give help for the benefit of others. This a very wonderful motivation that has inspired me to join the group. For as one grows older, the legacy to give help and share your time, talent and treasure to others makes my heart grow fonder" (11:52).

In addition to identifying Lions Clubs as an important aspect influencing members to engage in prolonged service activities, a second theme was the belief that service to humanity reflected a higher spiritual calling, as reflected in the following sample of responses: "I learned since I was a child that volunteering is the kindest act of love that exists. We are Lions. We help others and we don't expect anything in return. I thank God every day for the opportunity of helping people in need, for a better world" (8:40); "[Service] requires us to know that we are not getting anything in return. But, if you imagine how many people are being helped, the blessing that you are getting knowing that God is watching you, has no price" (10:35); "Even if you don't belong to any group, don't waste time. Engage in any activity, and I am sure that your life will get better, and one day you will be rewarded. God is watching you" (8:7); "Give thanks to God for being at the side of the people helping to make a change in this world" (10:42); "I feel I received a gift from God. God showed me I am on the right path. I have been a volunteer for 33 years" (8:82); "I believe that is extremely important that we share everything we receive from God with our less fortunate brothers. Give them the opportunity to smile, even for a short period of time" (8:89); "I feel like doing community service and helping others is how I receive strength from God" (10:30); "The reason that we should help each other is because it is a way of thanking God. To be at peace in this world and feeling happy. Seeing the smiles of the elderly that you helped and the innocent smiles of the kids playing" (10:66); "Working to help people makes you feel like you are giving part yourself to them. I think God gives us the opportunity to help others in need; to console or give your time to them helps you see life another way, knowing that you have something to live for" (10:89); and "I've been doing volunteer work of some kind since I was about ten years old. Every day I look for and find an opportunity to serve others. And at night, when I lay my head down upon my pillow, it's an awfully good feeling when I begin my talk with my God. And you know what? That smile is still there as I finish saying the last of my prayers and end with my final Amen" (11:42).

Conclusion

Reading or listening to stories from the heart is like opening a special box and finding a treasured item. We are captivated by the personal revelations and intimacy of the experience. While we may not fully comprehend the significance of the moments when individuals have experienced the epiphany of knowing that they will always be Lions, the value of the treasured experience is in the eyes of the storytellers and we empathize and share in the moment, anticipating our own life-changing experience. In the epilogue that follows, a look into the future provides a perspective on how an organization founded on service to others will endure.

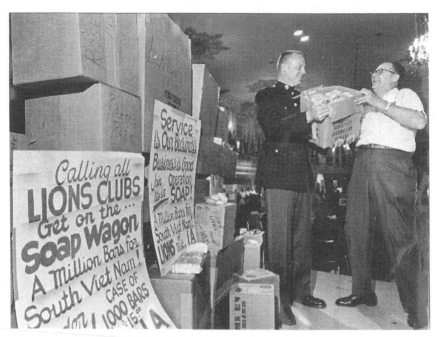

Collect 100 million bars of soap for South Vietnam 1966

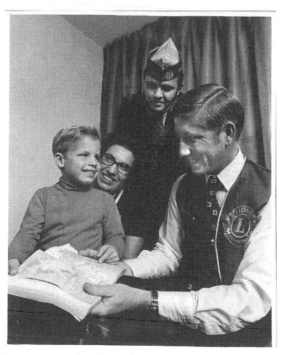

Lions Flown to England to observe child's eye operation 1971

Epilogue

"Lions is a great culture, and our purposes are realistic and relevant. I have a group that I can grow in and hopefully bring to it something of my own to enhance its continued value to our community." (11:11)

"The world is full of risky situations, misery, and injustice. For each problem we solve, many others appear. Our effort has to be constant. We cannot say we did our part, and now it is up to others to do theirs. We always have a challenge and we should always help." (8:63)

In 1895, H. G. Wells published a novel entitled, *The Time Machine*, where the central character—a scientist and inventor in Victorian England—purposely traveled into the distant future to observe how humankind had changed. Although the traveler was able to return to report on what he witnessed, his near escape from the future foreshadowed what may have befallen him on his second trip. The end of the story leaves the reader waiting for the return of the traveler, uncertain about his fate. While the reality of time travel has been elusive to scientists, the possibility of traveling through time has been a frequent subject for science fiction writers and the story of the time machine has fascinated the public in feature films, television shows, and comic books.

You may be wondering what time travel has to do with Lions Clubs and service, the focus of this book. Quite honestly, I often have wished that I could travel into the past to see and experience what it was like to live at another point in time. For me, one of those historical points of interest would be the time when a group of businessmen in Chicago, Illinois, USA came together and formed the International Association of Lions Clubs, later to become Lions Clubs International. Imagine what it must have been like in 1917 at the founding of this unique and impactful organization. What if you could travel back to that time in Chicago when the idea of serving the needs of others over self, became the basis for the creation of an international association? Watching the early Lions move among those in need would have been rewarding; and upon returning to the present, become part of my motivation for considering the story of H. G. Wells, along with stories of service from the hearts of Lions. In this epilogue, take a short trip to the past, fast forward to the future to consider how historians may describe LCI and the individuals who made service their mission, and then return to the present to acknowledge the opportunities and challenges facing the world at large, as well as the people who serve.

Chicago at the Turn of the 20th Century

Much has been written about conditions and circumstances in Chicago at the turn of the twentieth century when Lions Clubs International was born. According to historical accounts:

Chicago's economic dynamism between the 1850s and the 1920s is the stuff of legend.

> Seldom before in world history had an urban center grown so rapidly, being transformed so dramatically, or captured and conveyed the regnant spirit of the age so thoroughly ... Chicago had become America's industrial capital, there to remain for most of the twentieth century. (Coclanis, 2005)

As Chicago transformed itself into the second largest city in the United States and the heart of industrial production and manufacturing for the nation, the population grew dramatically.

Context is needed in order to understand what the demographic and societal transformation of Chicago must have been like. Into this industrial center of America came immigrants from rural areas of the Midwest and South. In addition, foreign immigration from Southern and Eastern Europe fueled Chicago's rise in population from just under 30,000 in 1850, to 2.2 million in 1910. By 1930, Chicago's population approached nearly four million (Coclanis, 2005). As the population increased, the economic, social, and structural systems supporting them experienced intense strain (Gordon, 1977). More housing, food, and services were needed.

Conditions were harsh and often entire families—men, women, and children—went to work in order to provide for their needs. As Hansan (2011) described: "poor parents or recent immigrants ... depended on their children's meager wages to survive." For the women and children, this meant working in the factories where they risked losing a finger or foot while tending unsafe equipment in the mills, being scalped if their hair got caught in open machinery, or being smothered or crushed by coal or other materials as they did their jobs. In spite of the dangers they faced, these workers had little difficulty getting a job, as they "were often preferred, because factory owners viewed them as more manageable, cheaper, and less likely to strike" (Child Labor, *n.d.*). As for the men, if they should be injured or happened to die, their wives and children were left with little recourse than to work in the factories (Gordon, 1977).

Health problems were often the result of unsanitary conditions and little was done to protect workers from disease and epidemics. As Nugent (2005) described: "The Board of Health lamented that 'the great and rapid influx of population has caused a dangerous overcrowding in all the poorer districts' ... Overcrowding produced deaths from tuberculosis as well as from sanitary-related contagions." Chicago residents suffered through disastrous epidemics including cholera and influenza. Conditions were worse for the blind, deaf, and disabled who were locked away in institutions or sterilized (This history of attitudes, *n.d.*) or featured in freak shows: "With freak shows, people with disabilities were often presented as savages from foreign countries" (Scholar uncovers hidden history, 1991).

The times were ripe for action in 1917, and into this environment came people like Melvin Jones to bring relief to the poor and destitute. There was a need and Lions were there to extend a helping hand. Imagine what it must have been like for affluent and successful Chicago businessmen and women in the community, to roll up their sleeves and intervene in the lives of men, women, and children needing food, support, educational opportunities at a time when most "middle and upper classes approached the problem with condescension, lack of understanding, and fears" (Gordon, 1977, p. 231). These early Lions provided programs for youth, citizenship training, health screenings, and worked to promote positive community development. The Lions provided services for the blind, deaf, and disabled and created opportunities for individuals to experience educational and recreational activities.

The growth of Lions' membership during this existence stage is evidence that people wanted to do something to change the circumstances facing the underserved. But not everyone possessed the agency to act upon their desire to help. Being educated and having financial resources was essential. While not a requirement of LCI, these characteristics of education and affluence were evident in the early membership of Lions Clubs as they spread to new territories and countries around the world. In these new areas, early adopters of Lionism were those with the means to enact change. During the maturity stage of LCI, when leaders were coordinating the establishment of new constitutional areas, educating new members about the importance of giving both time and personal wealth was promoted as a way to demonstrate the commitment to humanitarian service. When there was a disparity in a country or territory between those with resources and those without, the call to service placed the people with resources into the role of provider.

The State of the World in the Future

Fast forward to 2117 or beyond—maybe even 500 years into the future—and consider where and how Lions will be serving on the future centenary birthdays of their association. How will future historians record the work of Lions when they write about the founding and early phases of LCI in the twentieth century? How will they write about this period in history? Unlike other major movements that brought together great numbers of people in support of a particular cause, historians will need to write about Lions from a different viewpoint.

For example, unlike chronicling the political power of the great eastern dynasties and western empires, or explaining the rise of major spiritual or religious movements around the globe, historians won't be able to claim that Lions came together for political gain or religious dominance. We know this because according to the Lions International Objects,

"...partisan politics and sectarian religion shall not be debated by club members" (LCI Purpose, 2017). In other words, from the very beginning neither political motivation nor religious ardor served as motivation for individuals to serve the needs of the vulnerable in society through the cause of Lionism.

Similarly, historians won't write that Lions sought economic superiority or military might. Unlike the colonial powers that created economic empires and the powerful armies amassed by leaders seeking to control the destiny of millions, Lions over the past century have joined together to serve, rather than to rule. The Lions Code of Ethics reminds us of this mission, "to encourage service-minded people to serve their community without personal financial reward" and "to seek success ... but to accept no profit or success at the price of my own self-respect lost because of unfair advantage taken or because of questionable acts on my part" (LCI Purpose, 2017). Instead, Lions joined together from all cultures, religions, ethnicities, and backgrounds to meet humanitarian needs and to bring peace and international understanding to the world. This unique and universal call to social justice and equality transcends politics, religions, wealth, and might. These philosophical foundations are solid and have the capacity to last for generations to come.

Return to LCI in the Present

So, here we are back in the present. While the world dramatically has changed politically, economically, technologically, demographically, and socially, some of the same core needs that existed in 1917 when the founders created the association are present today. Specifically, these needs include: Sight and health-related issues, such as blindness, diabetes, and climate-related diseases; challenges for youth development and empowerment; food and water for the hungry; and protection of the local and global environment.

While progress has been made, sight-related needs such as cataract surgeries and tissue transplants are still present in many parts of the world. Preventing Trachoma, onchocerciasis (river blindness), and other overlooked tropical diseases that continue to plague the lives of hundreds of thousands of people in developing countries remains a priority. Young people may no longer be working in the factories, but they face challenges in the social arena in the form of bullying, drug abuse, and human trafficking. While some nations have a food surplus, millions of people around the world live in poverty and extreme forms of malnutrition and physical hardship continue to plague governments attempting to care for their people. Finally, the global environment is constantly challenged as water, air, and land pollution remain as significant issues affecting every continent around the world. The times in 2017 are ripe for action, and Lions are present to meet the needs in 210 countries and territories.

Takeaways for Thought and Action

The focus of this book has steadfastly centered on the stories of Lions as they realized that they would always be committed to serving the needs of vulnerable people in their communities and around the world. The inclusion of as many stories as possible has been rewarding and revealing, offering insight into the organizational development of Lions Clubs International and the personal development of individual Lions. But, added to this has come a more robust understanding of why Lions Clubs persist and continue to motivate individuals to volunteer their time and financial support to fulfill the motto: *We Serve!* The following takeaways weave together the stories and what they tell us about the future of Lions Clubs International.

Lions are Committed to Renewal

From the early founders to the current leadership, the focus over the first one hundred years on continually improving the organizational structure of the association in order to provide service for more people has enabled LCI to successfully move through the stages of existence, survival, maturity, and renewal. The decline stage has been avoided thus far because leaders have not allowed the structure of the organization to overtake its mission of providing service. Many examples support this claim, providing evidence of LCI's early and sustained commitment to organizational renewal.

One example occurred during the survival stage when the economy failed, signaling the start of the Great Depression. Lions Clubs were encouraged to suspend dues if necessary in order to retain their members and to continue providing service to those in greater need than themselves. The records show that LCI remained solvent during this period and membership actually grew because helping those in need motivated and inspired continued service. Another example can be drawn from the ashes of World War II. Lions Clubs encouraged patriotism and peace, providing assistance for soldiers and their families as well as for victims of the devastation of war. After the war when the world sought successful models of international peace and cooperation, LCI was among the few organizations invited to be part of the formation of the United Nations. This organizational relationship between LCI and the United Nations continues to demonstrate the benefit of partnerships in promotion of sustainable goals for the future of the world. There are many more such examples, but they all demonstrate the same finding: When difficulties have presented themselves, Lions have been challenged to strive on, providing service to their communities and those in need.

Lions Keep the Focus on Service

Throughout its history, LCI has kept service as its focus in the creative, directional, coordinated, and collaborative phases of Lionism. Service to others was the basis for the belief espoused by Melvin Jones that you can't get very far in life until you do something for somebody else. As he expanded his recruitment efforts, it was this belief in service that separated LCI from the other business and social clubs of the era. Throughout its first one hundred years, the willingness to volunteer and provide service has attracted millions of people to join Lions Clubs and begin their lifelong commitment to helping others. While service has remained central to Lionism, examples illustrate how Lions Clubs increased their impact through different phases of development.

Initially, when the founders organized the first clubs into an association, they allowed for local creativity when encouraging Lions to serve. Whether they served the blind or the physically challenged, children or families facing hardships associated with poverty and disease, or communities needing infrastructure and programs for immigrants and vulnerable publics, Lions developed projects to address these specific needs. Once established, Lions Clubs were receptive to direction from the international association about specific causes needing support. Helen Keller provided one such call to serve the blind and visually impaired. This call mobilized Lions Clubs and provided direction that has been sustained for nearly a century. Later, as LCI matured and spread around the world following World War II, it needed to establish programs to help guide the new Lions Clubs as they took on more and more service. Additionally, through a coordinated approach, Lions Clubs International Foundation began raising funds and awarding grants to assist local clubs and districts as they sponsored major projects to help those in need. Over the past thirty years, the creation of partnerships with public and private entities—for example, the Measles Initiative with GAVI and the Trachoma and River Blindness Project with The Carter Center—has demonstrated a collaborative approach to service. Throughout all of these phases, the centrality of service has remained at the core of Lionism.

Lionism is a Culture

The fact that culture is ubiquitous should surprise no one. Culture is everywhere we look: In the way people speak, dress, and present themselves; in the way relationships are formed; in the norms and values people espouse; and in way people see themselves in the world. Previous research has revealed that people in different geographic regions and contexts experience approaches to service that are quite varied. However, while approaches to service may vary and be culturally determined, a common culture of Lionism exists. This common culture unites all Lions from around the world.

The common elements of a culture of Lionism have been learned and sustained through local Lions Clubs. Three of these cultural elements include the language used to communicate; the intent of the perceived relationship between the volunteer and the recipient of the assistance; and the worldview of the volunteer to change the situation for the better. The stories of Lions illustrated these elements: Language in the form of words was not needed in order for Lions to communicate their feelings with each other or their genuine concern for those they served; the inherently positive intent of the relationship between Lions and those they served was to be helpful; and the worldview of Lions reflected the power and servant leadership associated with taking action to improve the lives of those in need.

One element, while positive was confounded in that it supported the giving of time and resources to assist those in need despite a tension about where that support from Lions Clubs should be placed. Specifically, the tension between Lions Clubs supporting only those people who were known to them versus Lions Clubs supporting anyone in need—known individuals as well as strangers from different countries—provided differentiation between Lions Clubs worldwide. For example, some Lions Clubs choose to focus solely on their local communities, while other Lions Clubs accept a global responsibility, supporting LCIF and projects beyond their city limits, helping people with different norms, beliefs, and values. In spite of these different perspectives, the culture of Lionism was revealed in the stories and provided a universal orientation that can be translated across ethnic and geographic borders.

Volunteers Join Lions Clubs for Different Reasons

According to the findings from the survey informing this book, people have been drawn to service for six different reasons, including: Service reflects my personal identity; service is part of my family heritage; service provides access for me to social connections; service increases my personal satisfaction about life; service makes others feel better physically, socially, and psychologically; and service helps to make the world a better place. These reasons were identified inductively from the responses the Lions provided when asked what motivated them to join a Lions Club and begin serving the needs of the vulnerable.

While these findings supported what scholars had written about why people affiliate with particular groups or organizations, a new finding of importance for Lions suggested that not all people chose to join a Lions Club for the same reasons. In fact, the motivation for one person may not be the same for another.

What did emerge from the findings was an awareness that despite cultural differences, these six reasons for joining a Lions Club were expressed across all of the participants. This reflected a universal orientation about the attractiveness of service to the broad membership of LCI. Additionally, from within the responses of each language were found these same service-related themes.

People Become and Remain Motivated to Serve in Meaningful Ways

People initially decided to provide service to the poor and vulnerable for several reasons. For example, service can help volunteers to understand what is happening in the world and why they are needed. Service may reflect the values of the volunteer, in addition to providing protection from self-recrimination due to guilt about not being as destitute as those being helped. Some people provide service because they believe their efforts will be noticed, thereby increasing their value in the beholder's eyes. The social side of making friends in Lions Clubs provides another motivational factor for those who want to participate in service and club activities. Finally, the opportunity to enhance the lives of those who receive assistance is compelling to most volunteers. While each of these reasons may be enough to motivate people to join a Lions Club, they often work in conjunction with each other. Furthermore, the more satisfaction the volunteer gets from these opportunities to serve, the more likely she will be to continue her participation in the Lions Club. In other words, only if the service continues to be meaningful will the volunteer continue to be involved. Similarly, when recruiting individuals to engage in service projects, Lions will use the activities that motivated them when they were deciding to join a Lions Club. These reasons often represent their prime motivation for maintaining their current level of involvement.

Lions Confirm the Call to Service Through Stories from the Heart

The one hundred selected stories highlighted in this book were revealing and personal. Many Lions shared deeply intimate moments when they opened their hearts to someone in need and their feelings were met with the rewarding response from the recipient. These stories from the heart were telling and reflected meaningful experiences that impacted their lives and the lives of the recipients. They were stories of action where intangible gifts were given and received as the service was rendered. The stories were inspiring and created a history of what Lionism has meant to people in need around the world.

While not generalizable, the emergent themes of these stories painted the picture of a common cultural orientation bound by empathy—the ability to feel the experience of another—and experienced one life at a time. Once felt, these stories remained as important reasons why volunteers continued their commitment to service.

Conclusion

When H. G. Wells published *The Time Machine*, he did more than stimulate thought about the potential of time travel. Through his futuristic characters representing two groups—the Eloi and the Morlocks—he illustrated to the time traveler what might happen in the future if the Eloi became too complacent about societal problems. When the Eloi became unable to control the power of the Morlocks, their ability to function was destroyed. Their deadly conflict demonstrated what would happen if people did not remain vigilant in confronting the powerful challenges they faced.

Lions in the twenty-first century face challenges with the capacity to destroy lives and livelihoods. Through service, LCI has remained vigilant in confronting these challenges. But the vigilance has come not from extrinsic sources. Rather, strength has been forthcoming from within the hearts of the volunteers who have given of their time and resources to help the most vulnerable and needy in the world. These stories have revealed the truth of what has made Lions Clubs International the largest service organization in the world: You don't get very far until you start doing something for somebody else.

Acknowledgments

This project started with the personal and financial support of many people and entities. First and foremost, I must thank the hundreds of Lions from around the world who shared their personal stories of epiphany when they knew in their hearts that they would always be committed to serving the needs of others. In addition to their stories, they offered their perspectives about what motivated them to serve, kept them serving, and how they recruited others to join them in service. I am in their debt for sharing what they have held in their hearts.

Lions Clubs International (LCI) endorsed the original project early in the process. This support changed its magnitude, transforming my initial survey into a global inquiry about what motivates Lions to serve. To gather data globally, LCI staff translated the survey from English into ten other official languages so that Lions could answer in their native languages. Using the email database of LCI, targeted online surveys and other email messages were disseminated worldwide. My esteem and gratitude is unmeasurable about the immediate and steady support provided by Dane LaJoye, Public Affairs Manager for LCI. He was instrumental in not only encouraging me, but authorizing and providing the necessary resources to move the project forward through the research and publication process. Scott Drumheller (former LCI Executive Administrator), Past International President J. Frank Moore III (Centennial Chairperson and Interim LCI Executive Administrator), and Rebecca Daou (LCIF Executive Administrator) were encouraging as the project moved ahead. Additionally, Sanjeev Ahuja (Chief of Marketing and Membership), Diane Keller (Global Strategy), and Mary Bartucci (Public Affairs) provided access to specific historical documents and other materials and services at LCI international headquarters. Other staff members at LCI provided encouragement and interest in the project, helping to sustain my commitment to complete the project.

My academic anchors, initially North Dakota State University in Fargo and later, the University of Central Florida in Orlando, provided access to library resources and support personnel. At NDSU, my appreciation is extended to the following: The Institutional Review Board for approving the procedures used to conduct the research; Linda Charlton-Gunderson of the Group Decision Center for programming the eleven translated questionnaires into a qualtrics online survey format; and Jade Monroe, a graduate student in the Department of Communication for masterfully coordinating the collection, translation, and management of the data. Jade's commitment to the project exceeded expectations, particularly as she worked with the international students and faculty who translated the responses from native language to English. The opportunity to work with Jade and watch her grow as a Lion was rewarding. At UCF, Emily Knapp, a master's graduate student in the Nicholson School of Communication was especially helpful in gathering and drafting reports of existing research on cultural perspectives associated with service in chapter 3; and the coding of the participant responses for chapters 3, 4, and 6. Another graduate student at UCF, Kelly Merrill assisted with the coding of data for chapter 4.

Finally, I must extend my personal appreciation to friends and fellow Lions. When I conceived of the idea to write a book about global service, Lions from Multiple District 5 (North Dakota, Saskatchewan, and South Dakota) encouraged me and never doubted my ability to complete the project. For fear of leaving someone out, let me say that those closest to me know how much I appreciated their ongoing support throughout the process. As I transitioned onto the International Board of Directors in 2014 and experienced some time constraints due to increased travel and juggling of responsibilities, my fellow directors inspired me to continue writing and moving forward with the project. The timing of the LCI Centennial and the fiftieth anniversary of Lions Clubs International Foundation in 2017 became the target date for completion, with LCIF as the sole beneficiary of any financial gain associated with this project.

My wife and partner-in-service, Lion Kathy deserves my sincere appreciation because she read every chapter, challenged me to clarify, and provided helpful comments to focus my thoughts and sharpen my writing.

She understood throughout the process how important it was for me to complete this project; and she made it possible for me to have the time to research and write when it was most convenient for me. Her love and confidence in me fueled my commitment and enabled me to produce this legacy project for the Centennial of our association.

When completed, this book represented hundreds of hours of time spent thinking, researching, writing, proofreading, and editing. Fortunately, the AuthorHouse Publishing Team, particularly Janice Cantrell and Era Lazaro, found value in a second edition; and now, I must acknowledge their good sense in bringing these stories of service to a larger audience. I could not have done this without their support. They rightfully deserve credit for tying a second bow on this centennial gift to Lions International.

—R. S. L.

References

Foreword

A History of the Heart. (*n.d.*) Retrieved from
    https://web.stanford.edu/class/history13/earlysciencelab/body/
    heartpages/heart.html

Berg, R. (2001, January 13). http://www.phrases.org.uk/bulletin board/7/
    messages/388.html

Cambridge Dictionary. (2024). Cambridge University Press & Assessment.
    Retrieved from
    https://dictionary.cambridge.org/us/dictionary/english/come-from-
    the-heart

Sebastian, L. (2016, April 27). Retrieved from
    https://www.quora.com/Whats-the-origin-of-the-phrase-from-the-
    bottom-of-my-heart

The Free Dictionary. (2024). Farlex, Inc. Retrieved from
    http://www.thefreedictionary.com/from+the+heart

Introduction

American Psychological Association. (2010). *Publication manual of the American Psychological Association* (6th ed.). Washington, DC: American Psychological Association.

Chapter 2

Aweida, G. S. (1997). *The pillars of Lionism*. Beirut, Lebanon: District 351.

Billings, M. (2005). The influenza pandemic of 1918. Retrieved from http://virus.sandord.edu/uda.

Casey, R., & Douglas, W. A. S. (1949). *The world's biggest doers.* Chicago, IL: Wilcox & Follett Co.

Copp, J. (2007, January). *The LION Magazine, 89*(6). Oak Brook, IL: Lions Clubs International.

Drumheller, S., & Cherep, S. (2016). LCI Forward: Strategic Plan 2015—2016 to 2019—2020. Retrieved from www.lionsclubs.org/resources/EN/ppt/LCI forward.ppt.

Greiner, L. (1972). Evolution and revolution as organizations grow. *Harvard Business Review*, 37—46.

Hadley and Its Partners. (2017). Hadley Institute for the Blind and Visually Impaired. Retrieved from www.hadley.edu/Partners.asp

Join the Centennial Service Challenge: 153,902,262 people served. (2017). Lions Clubs International. Retrieved from http://www.lions100.lionsclubs.org/EN/programs/centennial-service-challenge/index.php

Kleinfelder, R., & Brennan, D. (*n.d.*) An ideal triumphant. Unpublished manuscript.

Lester, D., Parnell, J., & Carraher, S. (2003). Organizational life cycle: A five-stage empirical scale. *Journal of Organizational Analysis, 11*(4), 339—354.

LCIF. (2017, June 12). Grants Approved between 1/1/1970 and 6/12/2017 (Report LA0062, Lions Clubs International Foundation. Oak Brook, IL: Lions Clubs International.

Martin, P. (1991). *We serve: A history of the Lions Club.* Washington, D.C.: Regnery Gateway.

Martin, P., & Kleinfelder, R. (2008). *Lions Clubs in the 21st Century.* Bloomington, IN: AuthorHouse.

Presidential Themes. (2017). Lions Clubs International. Retrieved from LCI O:\PublicRelations& Communications\PublicRelations\Admin\ PIPThemes\PresidentialThemes.Doc

Chapter 3

Assié-Lumumba, N. (2016). Evolving African attitudes to European education: Resistance, pervert effects of the single system paradox, and the ubunto framework for renewal. *International Review of Education /Internationale Zeitschrift Fur Erziehungswissenschaft, 62*(1), 11—27.

Bidee, J., Vantilborgh, T., Pepermans, R., Huybrechts, G., Willems, J., Jegers, M., Hofmas, J. (2013). Autonomous motivation stimulates volunteers' work effort: A self-determination theory approach to volunteerism. *Voluntas, 24*(1), 32—47. doi: 10.1007/s11266-012-9269-x

Breed, G., & Semenya, D. K. (2015). Ubuntu, koinonia and diakonia, a way to reconciliation in South Africa? *Hts, 71*(2), 1—9. doi: 10.4102/ hts.v7li2.2979

Brunell, A. B., Tumblin, L., & Buelow, M. T. (2014). Narcissism and the motivation to engage in volunteerism. *Current Psychology, 33*(3), 365—376. doi: 10.1007/s12144-014-9216-7

Brzozowski, J. C. (2013). From paid work to volunteerism during one case of natural disaster: Interacting micro and macro level transitions. *Work, 44*(1), 85—88. doi:10.3233/WOR-2012-01566

Chen, L. (2015). Rethinking successful aging: Older female volunteers' perspectives in Taiwan. *Asian Journal of Women's Studies, 21*(3), 215—231. doi:http://dx.doi.org.ezproxy.net.ucf.edu/10.1080/12259276.2015.1072939

Chong, A. L., Rochelle, T. L., & Liu, S. (2013). Volunteerism and positive aging in Hong Kong: A cultural perspective. *International Journal of Aging & Human Development, 77*(3), 211—231. doi:http://dx.doi.org.ezproxy.net.ucf.edu/10.2190/AG.77.3.c

Clary, E. G., Snyder, M., Ridge, R. D., Copeland, J., Stukas, A. A., Haugen, J., & Miene, P. (1998). Understanding and assessing the motivations of volunteers: A functional approach. *Journal of Personality and Social Psychology, 74*(6), 1516.

Dageid, W., Akintola, O., & Sæberg, T. (2016). Sustaining motivation among community health workers in AIDS care in Kwazulu-Natal, South Africa: Challenges and prospects. *Journal of Community Psychology, 44*(5), 569. doi:10.1002/jcop.21787

Dieckmann, A., Grimm, V., Unfried, M., Utikal, V., & Valmasoni, L. (2016). On trust in honesty and volunteering among Europeans: Cross-country evidence on perceptions and behavior. *European Economic Review.* doi:10.1016/j.euroecorev.2016.01.011

Elrod, L. P. (2013). Volunteering. *Salem Press Encyclopedia.*

Finkelstien, M. A. (2009). Intrinsic vs. extrinsic motivational orientationss and the volunteer process. *Personality and Individual Differences, 46*(5)

Guy, D. J. (2009). *Women build the welfare state: Performing charity and creating rights in Argentina, 1880-1955.* Durham, NC: Duke University Press.

John, L. B. E. (2015). Exploring Ubuntu discourse in South Africa: Loss, liminality, and hope. *Verbum Et Ecclesia, 2,* 1. doi:10.4102/VE.V36I2.1427

Lim, C., & MacGregor, C. A. (2012). Religion and volunteering in context: Disentangling the contextual effects of religion on voluntary behavior. American Sociological Review, 5, 747.

Lipford, J. W., & Yandle, B. (2009). The determinates of purposeful volunteerism. *The Journal of Socio-Economics, 38*(1), 72—79. doi:http://dx.doi.org/10.1016/j.socec.2008.10.012

Minutes of Meeting of Representatives from Various Business Men's Clubs. (1917, June 7). Archived at Lions Clubs International headquarters in Oak Brook, Illinois.

Moreno-Jiminez, M., & Villodres, M. (2010). Prediction of burnout in volunteers. *Journal of Applied Social Psychology, 40,* 1798—1818.

Prouteau, L., & Sardinha, B. (2015). Volunteering and country-level religiosity: Evidence from the European Union. *Voluntas: International Journal of Voluntary and Nonprofit Organizations, 1,* 242. doi:10.1007/s11266-013-9431-0

Ruiter, S., & DeGraaf, N. D. (2006). National context, religiosity, and volunteering: Results from 53 countries. *American Sociological Review, 71*(2), 191—210.

Serwah, A. (2011). Holding on to African values. *New African, 506,* 76-77.

Swartz, A., & Colvin, C. J. (2015). 'It's in our veins': Caring natures and material motivations of community health workers in contexts of economic marginalization. *Critical Public Health, 25*(2), 139—152. doi:10.1080/09581596.2014.941281

Themudo, N. S. (2009). Gender and the nonprofit sector. *Nonprofit and Voluntary Sector Quarterly, 38*(4), 663—683. doi:10.1177/0899764009333957

Wahrendorf, M., Blane, D., Matthews, K., & Siegrist, J. (2016). Linking quality of work in midlife to volunteering during retirement: A European study. *Journal of Population Aging, 1-2*, 113. doi:10.1007/s12062-015-9129-8

Warburton, J., & Winterton, R. (2010). The role of volunteering in an era of cultural transition: Can it provide a role identity for older people from Asian cultures? *Diversity (14242818), 2*(8), 1048. doi:10.3390/d2081048

Weinstein, N., & Ryan, M. (2010). When helping helps: Autonomous motivation for prosocial behavior and its influence on well-being for the helper and recipient. *American Psychological Association, 98*(2), 222—244. doi:10.1037/a0016984

Woitha, K., Hasselaar, J., van Beek, K., Radbruch, L., Jaspers, B., Engels, Y., & Vissers, K. (2015). Volunteers in palliative care—A comparison of seven European countries: A description study. *Pain Practice, 15*(6), 572—579. doi:10.1111/papr.12209

Chapter 4

Casey, R., & Douglas, W. A. S. (1949). *The world's biggest doers: The story of the Lions.* Chicago, IL: Wilcox & Follett Co.

Clary, E. G., & Snyder, M. (1999). The motivations to volunteer: Theoretical and practical considerations. *Current Directions in Psychological Science, 8*(5), 156—159.

Clary, E. G., Snyder, M., Ridge, R. R., Copeland, J., Stukas, A. A., Haugen, J., & Miene P. (1998). Understanding and assessing the motivations of volunteers: A functional approach. *Journal of Personality and Social Psychology, 74*(6), 1516—1530.

Curtis, J. E., Grabb, E., & Baer, D. (1992). Voluntary association membership in fifteen countries: A comparative analysis. American Sociological Review, 57, 139—152.

daSilva, Z. C. (2014). *Lions club: The great idea of Melvin Jones.* Indianapolis, IN: Dog Ear Publishing, LLC.

Kleinfelder, R., & Brennan, D. (*n.d.*) An ideal triumphant. Unpublished manuscript.

Martin, P. (1991). *We serve: A history of the Lions Clubs.* Washington, D.C.: Regnery Gateway.

Martin, P., & Kleinfelder, R. (2008). *Lions clubs in the 21ˢᵗ Century.* Bloomington, IN: AuthorHouse.

Moreno-Jimenez, M. P., & Villodres, M. C. H. (2010). Prediction of burnout in volunteers. *Journal of Applied Social Psychology, 40*(7), 1798—1818.

Chapter 5

Bruner, J. (1991, Autumn). The narrative construction of reality. *Critical Inquiry, 18*(1), 1—21.

Howell, W. S. (1982). *The empathic communicator.* Belmont, CA: Wadsworth Publishing Co.

Rogers, E. M. (2003). *Diffusion of Innovations* (5ᵗʰ ed.). New York: The Free Press.

Epilogue

Child Labor Public Education Project. (*n.d.*). Retrieved from https://www.continuetolearn.uiowa.edu/laborctr/child labor/about / us history.html

Coclanis, P. A. (2005). Business of Chicago. *The Electronic Encyclopedia of Chicago*. Chicago Historical Society. Retrieved from http://www. encyclopedia.chicagohistory.org/pages/198.html

Gordon, L. (1977, June). Women and the anti-child labor movement in Illinois, 1890—1920. *Social Service Review, 51*(2), 228—248.

Hansan, J. (2011). The American era of child labor. *Social Welfare History Project*. Retrieved from http://socialwelfare.library.vcu.edu/programs/ child-welfarechild-labor/child-labor/Supreme Court just two years later.

Lions Clubs International Purpose. (2017). Lions Clubs International. Retrieved from http://www.lionsclubs.org

Murphy, S. A. (2002, August 14). Life insurance in the United States through World War I. *EH.Net Encyclopedia*, edited by Robert Whaples. Retrieved fromhttp://en.net/encyclopedia/life-insurance-in-the-united-states-through-world-war-i/

Nugent, W. (2005). Epidemics. *The Electronic Encyclopedia of Chicago*. Chicago Historical Society. Retrieved from http://www.encyclopedia. chicagohistory.org/pages/432.html

Scholar uncovers hidden history of people with disabilities. (1991, May 15). Stanford University News Service. Stanford University, Stanford, CA. Retrieved from http://news.stanford.edu/pr/91/910515Arc1373.html

The history of attitudes to disabled people. (*n.d.*) The 19th Century. Retrieved from https://attitudes2disability.wordpress.com/2007/02/03/ the-19th-century/

Thompson, D. (2016, February 11). America in 1915: Long hours, crowded houses, death by trolly. *The Atlantic*. Retrieved from https://www. theatlantic.com/business/archive/2016/02/america-in-1915/462360/

Index

Printed in the United States
by Baker & Taylor Publisher Services